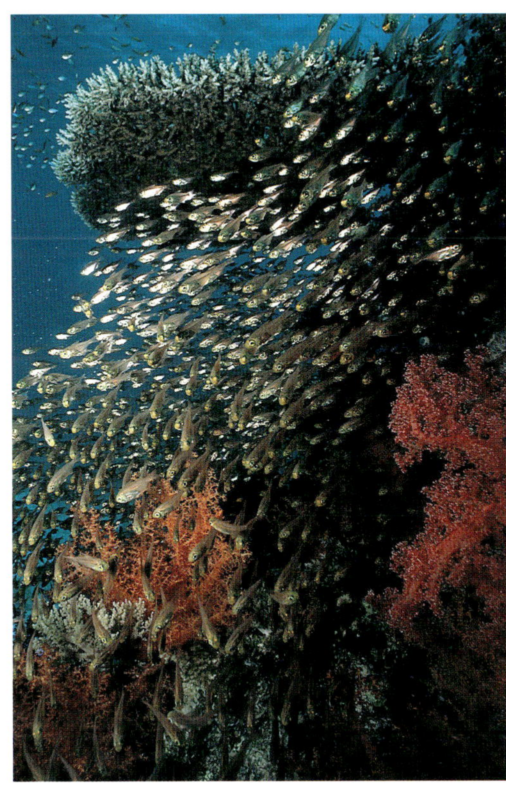

The Complete Guide to Photographing Underwater Wonders

Text and Photographs by Rick Sammon
Foreword by Emory Kristof, National Geographic Society

Voyageur Press

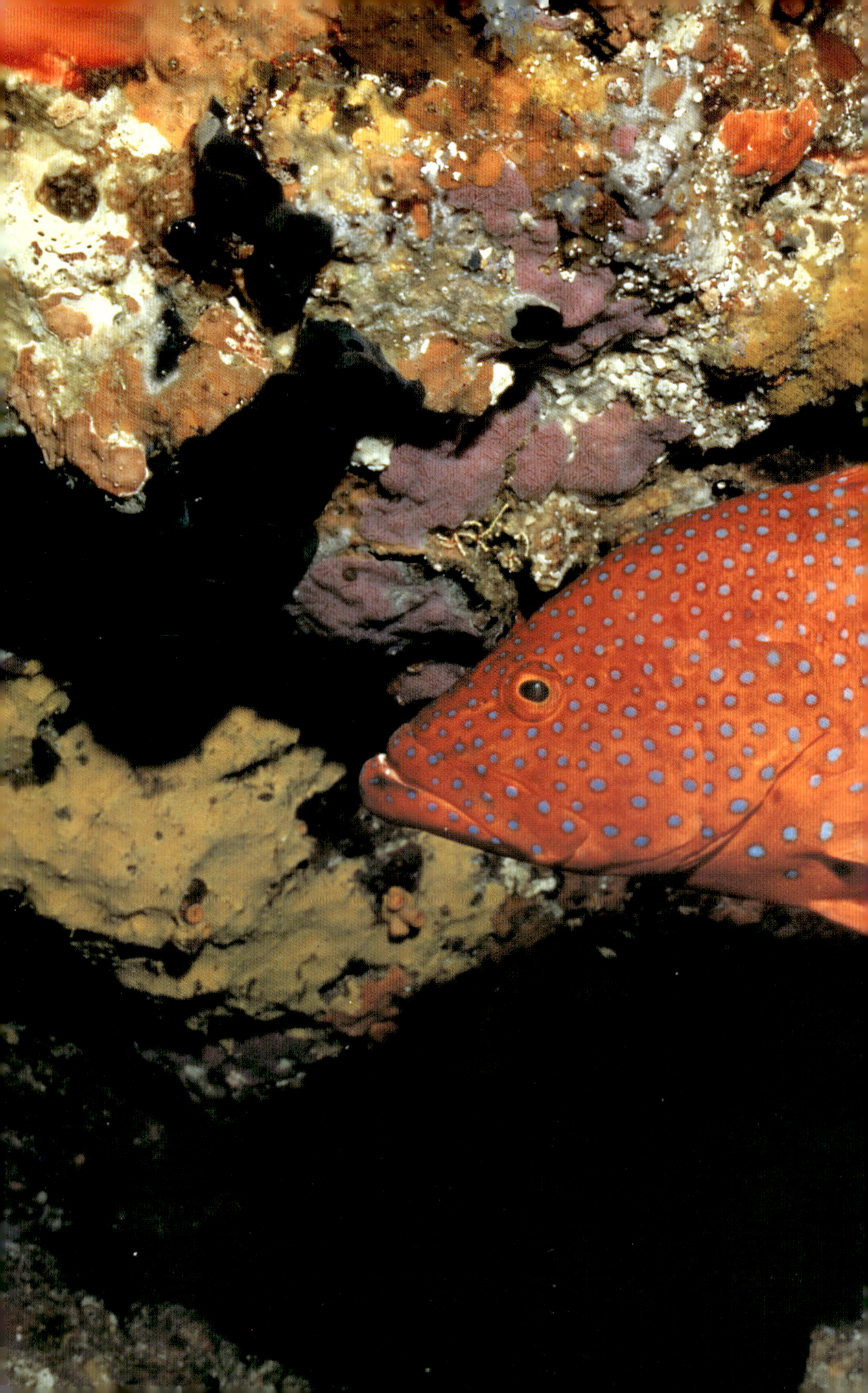

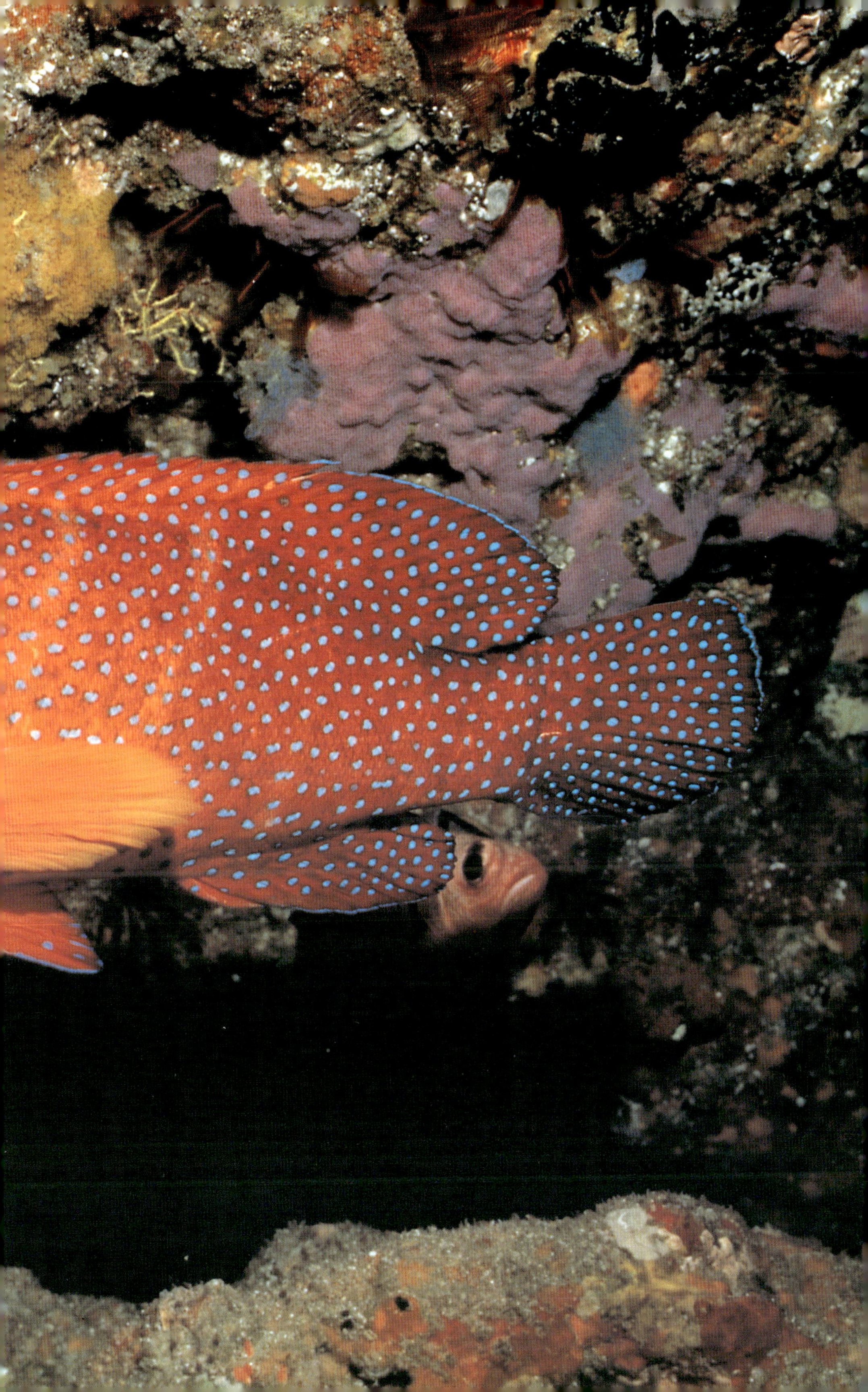

Edited by Mary Katharine Parks and Helene Anderson
Designed by Helene Anderson and Kathryn Mallien
Printed in Hong Kong
95   96   97   98   99   5   4   3   2   1

Library of Congress Cataloging-in-Publication Data
Sammon, Rick.
        The complete guide to photographing underwater wonders / Rick Sammon ;
foreword by Emory Kristof.
                p.   cm.
        Includes bibliographical references and index.
        ISBN 0-89658-252-3
        1. Underwater photography. I. Title.
        TR800.S25   1995
        778.7'3—dc20   94-31816
                                                              CIP

Distributed in Canada by Raincoast Books, 8680 Cambie Street, Vancouver, B.C. V6P 6M9

Published by Voyageur Press, Inc.
123 North Second Street, P.O. Box 338, Stillwater, MN 55082 U.S.A.
612-430-2210, fax 612-430-2211

Please write or call, or stop by, for our free catalog of natural history publications.
Our toll-free number to place an order or to obtain a free catalog is 800-888-WOLF (800-888-9653).

Educators, fundraisers, premium and gift buyers, publicists, and marketing managers: Looking for creative products and new sales ideas? Voyageur Press books are available at special discounts when purchased in quantities, and special editions can be created to your specifications. For details contact our marketing department.

PAGE 1: Photographing underwater wonders is a joy, as well as a challenge. **Subject:** Silversides on coral head. **Site:** Northern Red Sea, Egypt. **Equipment and film:** Nikonos V, Sea & Sea 15mm lens, two Nikonos SB-103 strobes, Kodachrome 64. PAGES 2–3: Chapter 13 discusses "thinking before you shoot." Here, when photographing colorful fish against equally colorful (and distracting) backgrounds, timing and depth-of-field control are crucial for a good picture. Here, the fish was photographed when it was swimming in front of a section of the reef that had subtle colors. In addition, a large *f*-stop provided shallow depth of field. **Subject:** Coral grouper. **Site:** South Africa. **Equipment and film:** Nikonos RS, 60mm macro lens, Nikonos SB-104 strobe, Kodachrome 64. BACK COVER: Rick and Susan Sammon at work. (Photo by Angela Anderson)

Dedicated to

My parents, who showed me the joy—and importance—of photography.

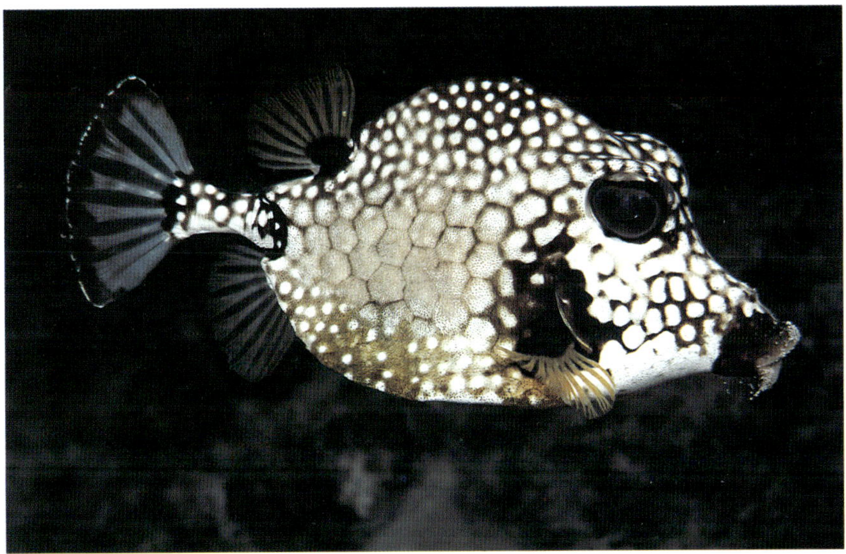

The Complete Guide to Photographing Underwater Wonders is written in easy-to-understand language, not high-tech talk. After reading the text, you'll be able to get great pictures—even on your first dive. **Subject:** Honeycomb cowfish. **Site:** Bonaire, Netherlands Antilles. **Equipment and film:** Nikonos RS, 50mm lens, Nikonos SB-103 strobe, Kodak Elite 100.

Contents

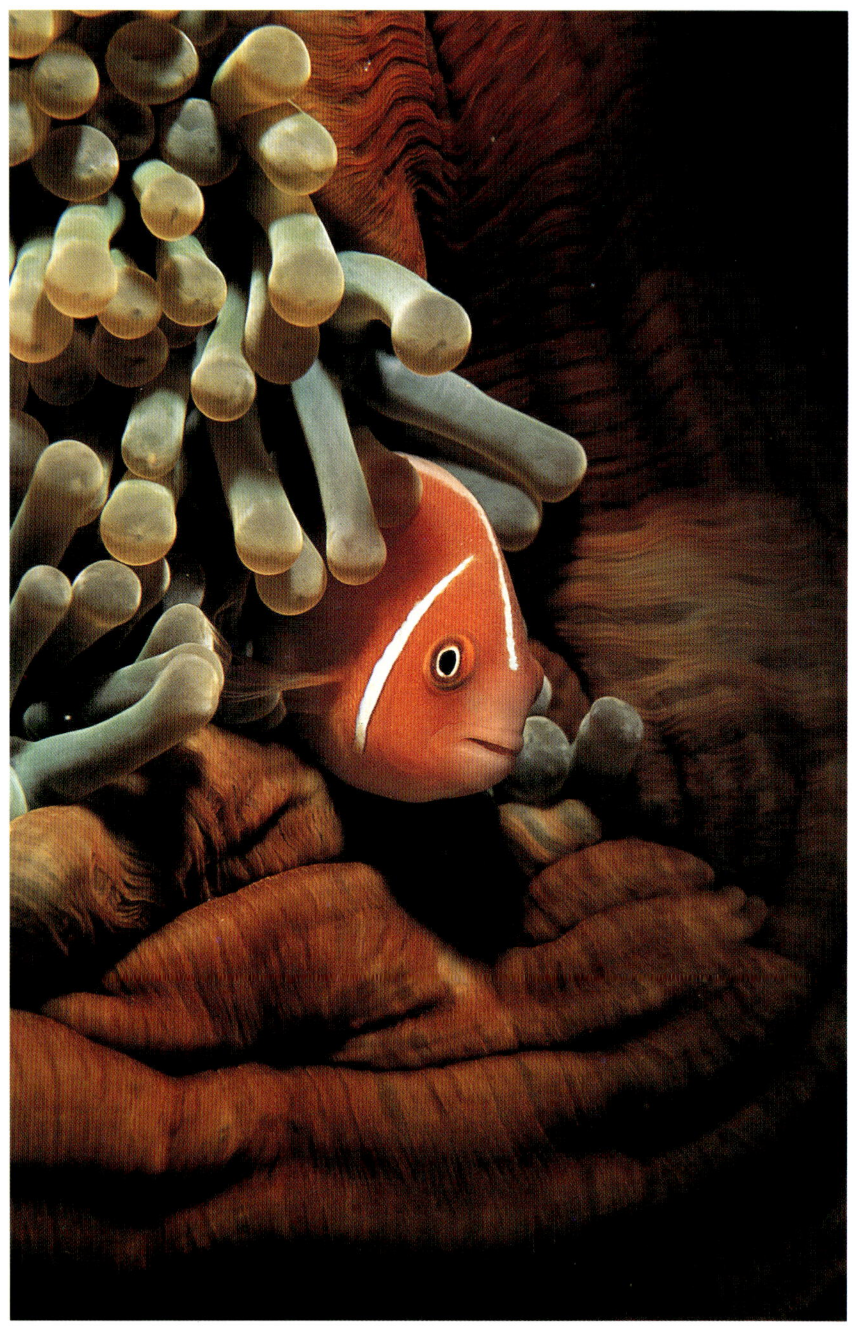

Subject: Clownfish in a sea anemone. **Site:** Fiji Islands, South Pacific. **Equipment and film**: Nikon 8008s, Stromm One underwater housing, 60mm lens, Nikonos SB-103 strobe, Kodachrome 64.

Foreword

Taking and sharing great underwater images makes diving even more thrilling. Let Rick Sammon be your guide.

Voyages to strange new worlds, floating in space, adventure! The siren song of Jacques Cousteau's "The Silent World" called to me as a young boy of the 1950s. The images from the historic Cousteau film led to my first thoughts of wanting to reverse the Darwinian march of biological progress and return to the sea. The images fired my imagination, and the making of those images became my life's work.

Underwater photography has challenges and requires disciplines unknown to land photography. While I don't think I would trade my experiences with a fish tank and a towel (my first underwater camera housing), the craft has come a long way in thirty-four years since I made my first soggy snaps. A good guide is what is needed, and Rick Sammon is one of the best.

As director of CEDAM International, an exploration organization dedicated to conservation, education, diving, archeology, and museums, Rick has led many world-ranging underwater expeditions. His pictures have been published everywhere. Several years ago it was my pleasure to have Rick and his wife, Susan, join me on a National Geographic project in Lake Baikal in Siberia. Their dry suits got a thorough workout in that frigid, crystalline, freshwater sea. The haunting pictures they took of the unique, green-sponge-dominated bottom, and the young freshwater seal under the three-foot-thick winter ice, appeared in their marvelous book, *Seven Underwater Wonders of the World*. I could afford to chuckle at their goose-bumps—I was doing my diving via a television link to a robot from the warmth of the boat's cabin.

Rick uses his experiences to communicate to others the lessons he has learned. His Associated Press column on photography reaches approximately 2.5 million readers each week. He is a regular contributor to *Rodale's Scuba Diving*, *Underwater USA*, and *Outdoor Photographer*. With this book, Rick takes the reader into the world of underwater photography and shortens the learning curve. There is no real reason to flounder around with home-built equipment and completely self-taught seat-of-the-pants technique. This is the nineties: the wet suits come in designer colors and cameras are no longer engineering nightmares that sorely test creative ability and patience. Let Rick make underwater photography fun! The reader may find what Rick and I already know—the taking and sharing of great underwater images is one of the best parts of diving.

—Emory Kristof,
National Geographic Society Staff Photographer

In this book, Rick Sammon shares underwater tips, tricks, and techniques, so you can turn snapshots (RIGHT) into great shots (OPPOSITE). **Subject:** Sunken rowboat. **Site:** Bonaire, Netherlands Antilles. **Equipment and film:** Nikonos V, 15mm lens, Nikonos SB-103 strobe, Kodak Elite 100.

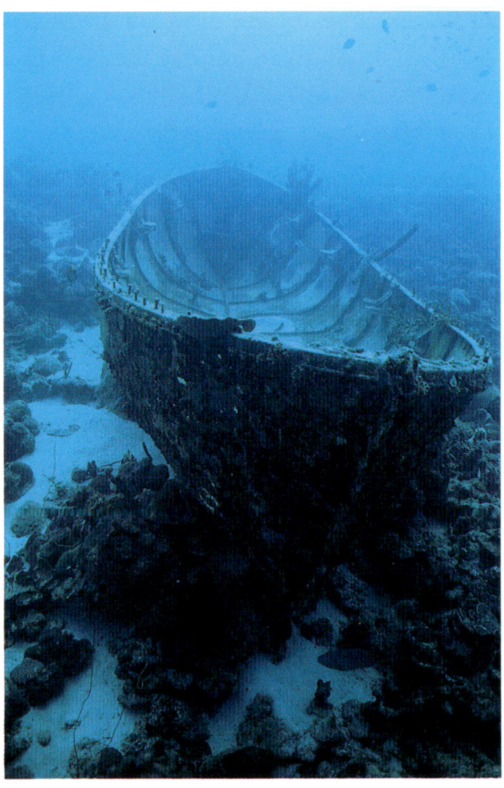

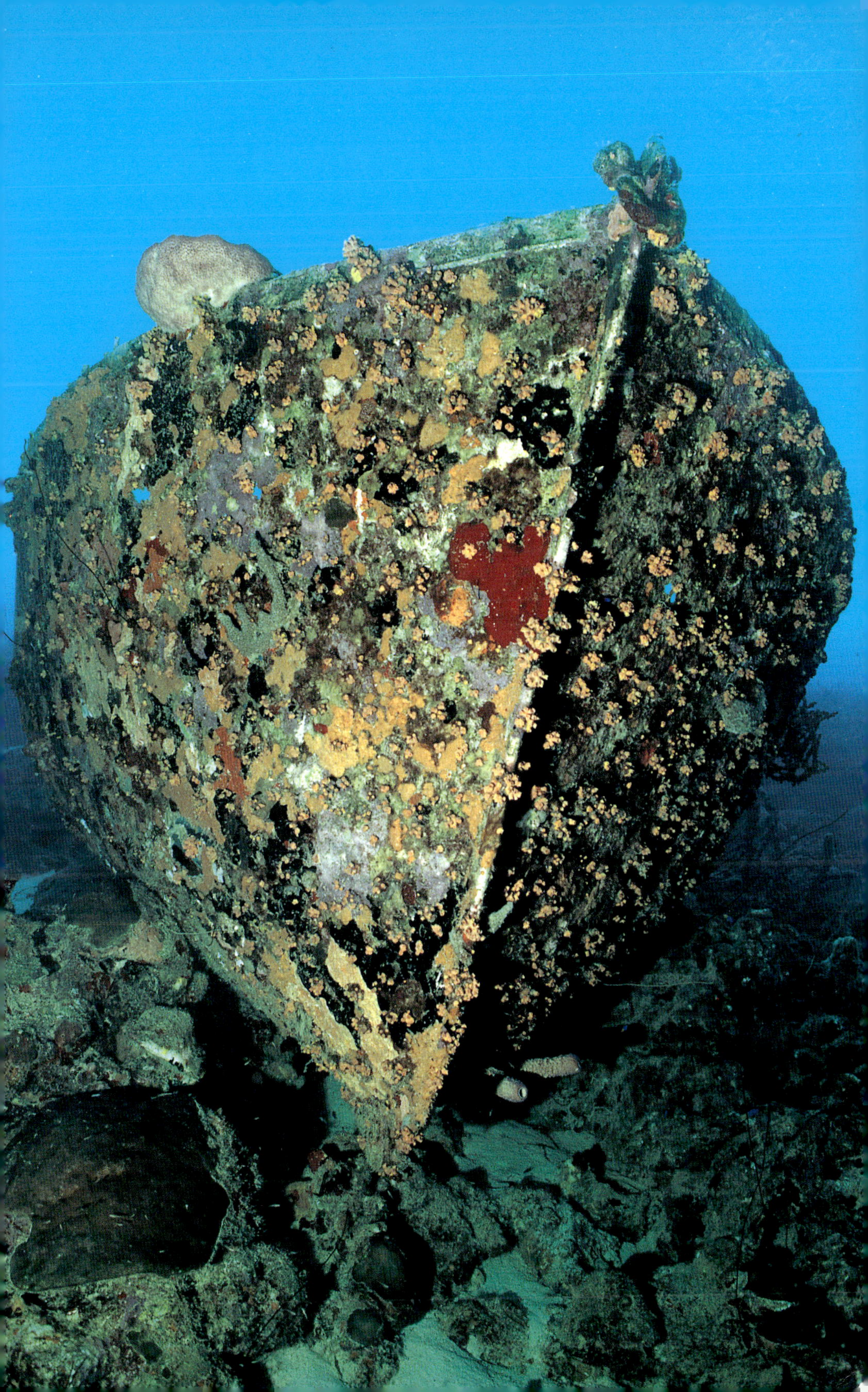

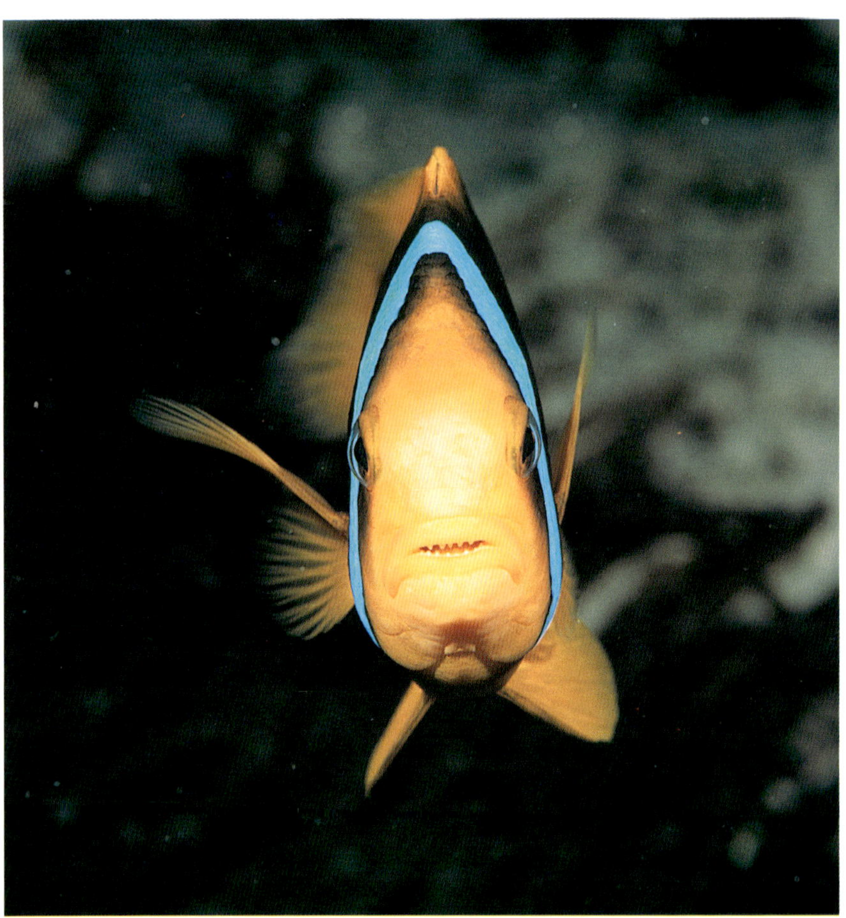

Underwater pictures bring back the excitement of scuba diving. They also help you share unique encounters with your friends and family. **Subject:** Clownfish in a sea anemone. **Site:** Fiji Islands, South Pacific. **Equipment and film:** Nikon 8008s, Stromm One underwater housing, 60mm macro lens, two Nikonos SB-103 strobes, Kodachrome 64.

Introduction: Dive In!

Explore the ocean realm with your camera and see some of the most awe-inspiring sites on our planet— some of the most exotic animals and plants, and underwater colors unlike any you've seen before.

Welcome to the rewarding and challenging world of underwater photography. As you explore the ocean realm with your camera, you'll see some of the most awe-inspiring sites on our planet and some of the most exotic animals. And when you dive with an underwater flashlight, you'll see colors unlike any you have seen before.

As an underwater explorer, you'll experience many things: adventure when you travel to exotic locations, amazement when you see a fish as big as a school bus, excitement when you plunge into pitch black water for a night dive, and a thrill when a school of sharks swims between you and your dive boat—even though you know most sharks pose no real threat to scuba divers.

When you get home from a dive vacation, your pictures help keep your memories fresh. On cold, rainy days, you'll find that your pictures will warm your spirit and inspire you to plan more trips so you can take more underwater pictures.

I've been passionate about underwater photography since 1980. Back then, my system comprised one manual exposure Nikonos camera, one 15mm lens, and one underwater strobe. I learned the versatility—as well as the limitations—of this very basic system. I worked hard at getting good pictures—some of which were good enough to get published and generate a few bucks.

Today, I have several underwater cameras, lots of lenses and accessories, and plenty of backup equipment. But, with all this gear and after all these years, I feel that it's not the latest-and-greatest camera equipment that makes a good underwater picture, it's how I record a particular scene or subject on film—in my own special way. For me, a good underwater picture is one that brings back a good memory, or lets me share an underwater moment with others.

Even with a one-camera/one-lens/one-strobe system, you can get some great underwater pictures, even on your first dive. Of course, if you are new to underwater photography, you'll need to learn some tips, tricks, and techniques to help you capture on film what you picture in your "mind's eye."

I've written this book with this end in mind. In *The Complete Guide to Photographing Underwater Wonders*, I've assumed that you have a basic knowledge of SLR (and "point-and-shoot") cameras and terminology. The glossary is there for a little assistance here and there, and I've listed some good basic photography books in case you're looking for more direction. *The Complete Guide to Photographing Underwater Wonders* then takes you the rest of the way. I hope it will give you a good understanding of underwater camera equipment, shooting techniques, and a respect for the ocean environment. Equipped with this knowledge, you'll be ready to successfully document the ocean realm as you see it. If you are lucky, you'll come back from your diving vacations with some pictures you'll be proud of.

But remember, as I always tell my underwater photography students: "The harder you work, the luckier you'll be."

Safe diving.

—**Rick Sammon,**
1995, Croton-on-Hudson, New York—
where I never go diving

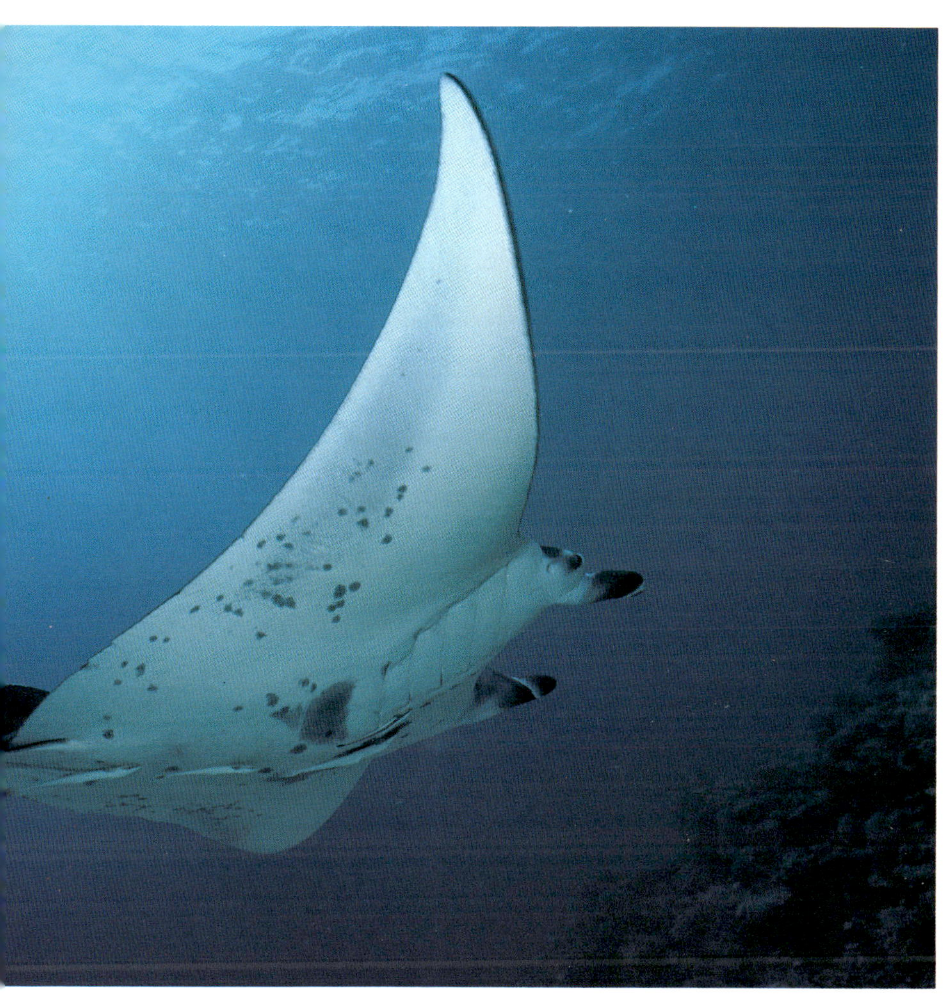

Luck plays an important role in underwater photography. However, being fully prepared for lucky situations is essential to getting good photographs. **Subject:** Manta ray. **Site:** Fiji Islands, South Pacific. **Equipment and film:** Nikonos V, Sea & Sea 15mm lens, Sea & Sea YS 200 strobe, Kodachrome 64.

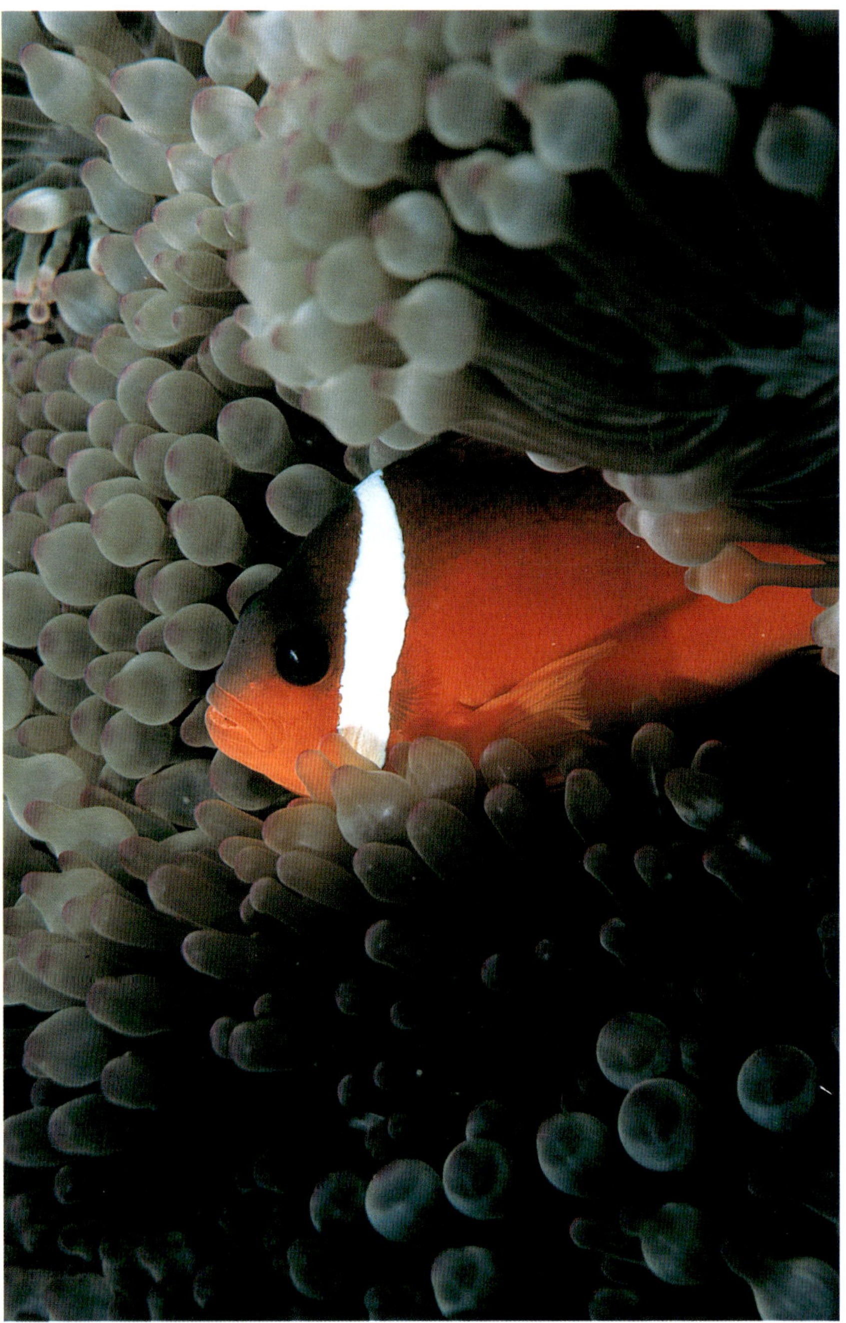

When photographing fast-moving fishes, a single-lens-reflex camera in an underwater housing or a system such as the Nikonos RS will let you see exactly what's in your frame. **Subject:** Tomato clownfish in a sea anemone. **Site:** Fiji Islands, South Pacific. **Equipment and film:** Nikon N8008s, Stromm One underwater housing, 60mm lens, Nikonos SB-103 strobe, Kodachrome 64.

Chapter 1: Building a Camera System

One of the first steps on the road to becoming a good underwater photographer is knowing what equipment you'll need—and can afford.

If you're just getting into scuba diving and taking pictures under water, I'd suggest starting with a basic system: one camera, one lens, and one strobe. "Keep it Simple," and you'll have fewer variables to worry about when looking through your camera's viewfinder.

After you begin to get good results, I'd suggest gradually adding lenses to your system. As each lens is added, work with that lens until you know its advantages and disadvantages.

Selecting that first system can be a difficult decision, because once you lock into a system, it's hard to change to another—emotionally and financially. So, read this chapter carefully to learn about the different systems that are available. Then, consider all factors and make your decision accordingly.

Underwater Housings for Your Existing "Topside" Camera System

Underwater housings for SLRs: Underwater camera housings are made of molded plastic, metal, or aluminum. Basically, they keep your on-land camera safe and dry while giving you access to the camera's controls. Shooting with a single-lens-reflex camera (SLR) in an underwater housing offers a practical advantage over underwater systems such as the Seamaster Pro and Nikonos V: You view the scene through the lens, so the scene you see in the viewfinder is the one you get on film. But perhaps the main advantage to an underwater housing is that you can use your topside SLR camera for underwater shooting, too.

One possible drawback to housings is that they are larger and heavier than a Nikonos V, which is about the size of an SLR.

Some of the metal and sturdy plastic housings offered by Canon, Ikelite, Aquatica, and Oceanic offer full control over focus, exposure, shutter speed, and *f*-stop via the regular manual controls on your topside camera. Others, like the Stromm One, accommodate only fully automatic models, though that is not necessarily a drawback. The Stromm One is designed for use with the Nikon N8008s, Canon EOS-1, and Minolta Maxxum 7000—all of which deliver excellent pictures in the autofocus/autoexposure mode. So, with a Stromm One housing, you can compose and shoot, too.

If you have a selection of lenses for your SLR, housing manufacturers offer lens ports that let you use individual lenses, from 6.5mm fisheye to 105mm macro.

New housings range in price from about $800 to $3,000.

Sea & Sea dedicated SLR and housing: In 1994, Sea & Sea introduced a unique camera and housing system called the SX-1000. The system consists of an SLR specifically designed for use in a compact and lightweight housing. Six different lenses are available, from 14mm to 180mm, including a 28–70mm zoom and two optical ports. Out of the housing, the SX-1000 SLR can be used for creative topside shooting, with any of the SX lenses.

This complete systems sells for about $3,500.

Flexible plastic housings: In addition to sturdy plastic and metal housings, less rugged, flexible plastic housings by EWA Marine are available for most 35mm SLRs and 35mm compact cameras. These inexpensive housings, ranging in price from about $70 to $180, offer a waterproof latch that keeps your camera and on-camera strobe safe and dry and an optical port for sharp pictures.

Underwater Cameras and Accessories

Nikonos V system: The manual focus Nikonos V system is perhaps the most popular underwater photography system available, for several reasons. First, the camera does not require an underwater housing, so you can operate all the controls under water, even while wearing diving gloves. Second, the following accessories add to the system's flexibility and versatility: interchangeable lenses (15mm super wide-angle, 20mm wide-angle, 35mm standard, and 80mm telephoto), Nikonos Close-up Kit and extension tubes — hollow, lensless tubes that fit between the lens and camera and offer greater-than-lifesize reproduction — for close-up photography. Also available are automatic and manual strobe units.

In addition, automatic flash and automatic available light exposure control on the Nikonos V offers "point and shoot" simplicity, while full manual exposure control offers unique creative possibilities.

The main disadvantage of the Nikonos V is that you view the scene through a viewfinder, and not through the lens. So, what you see is not exactly what you get on film.

A complete Nikonos V system will cost about $3,500.

Nikonos RS: The Nikonos RS is a 35mm autofocus SLR that is designed exclusively for underwater use. The list of features and benefits is impressive. First, the focusing system offers not one, but five focus modes:
* Single-Servo AF (autofocus) — the camera focuses on the subject and fires only when the subject is in focus, then advances the film one frame;
* Continuous-Servo AF — functions the same as the Single-Servo mode but the film is advanced as long as the shutter release button is depressed;
* Power Manual Focus — the camera can be focused manually via a rocker switch. This is useful in low-light situations when autofocusing is difficult;
* Freeze Focus — you pre-set the focus, and when a subject (fish or other marine animal) swims into the frame, the shutter is automatically released;
* Focus Tracking — the camera tracks a moving subject and fires anytime the shutter button is depressed.

A second feature of this system is that the camera offers aperture priority automation and manual exposure control. And there is even an exposure compensation dial that offers fine-tuning of exposure in one-third stops up to two stops over and two stops under the recommended setting.

Film handling is also simplified with the Nikonos RS. It is automatic, with single frame advance and auto rewind. This is good news for underwater photographers who have to change film on deck when a boat is rockin' and rollin' in heavy seas.

The Nikonos RS underwater system includes four lenses — 13mm,

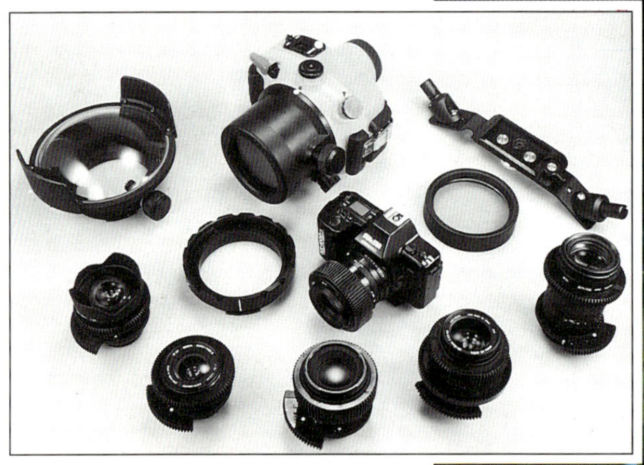

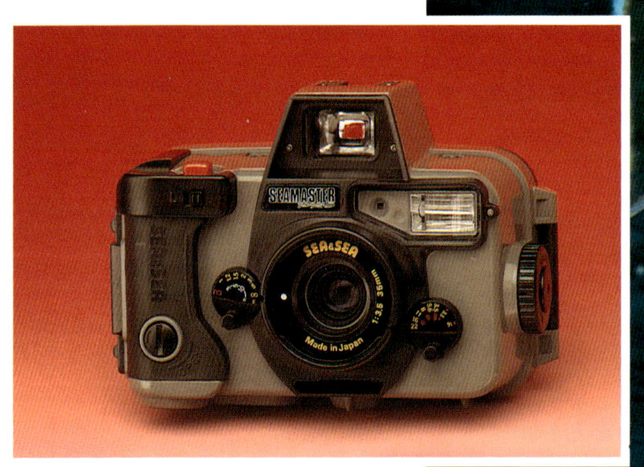

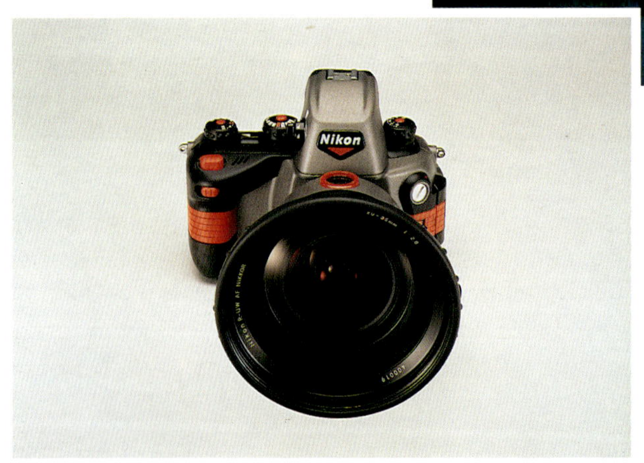

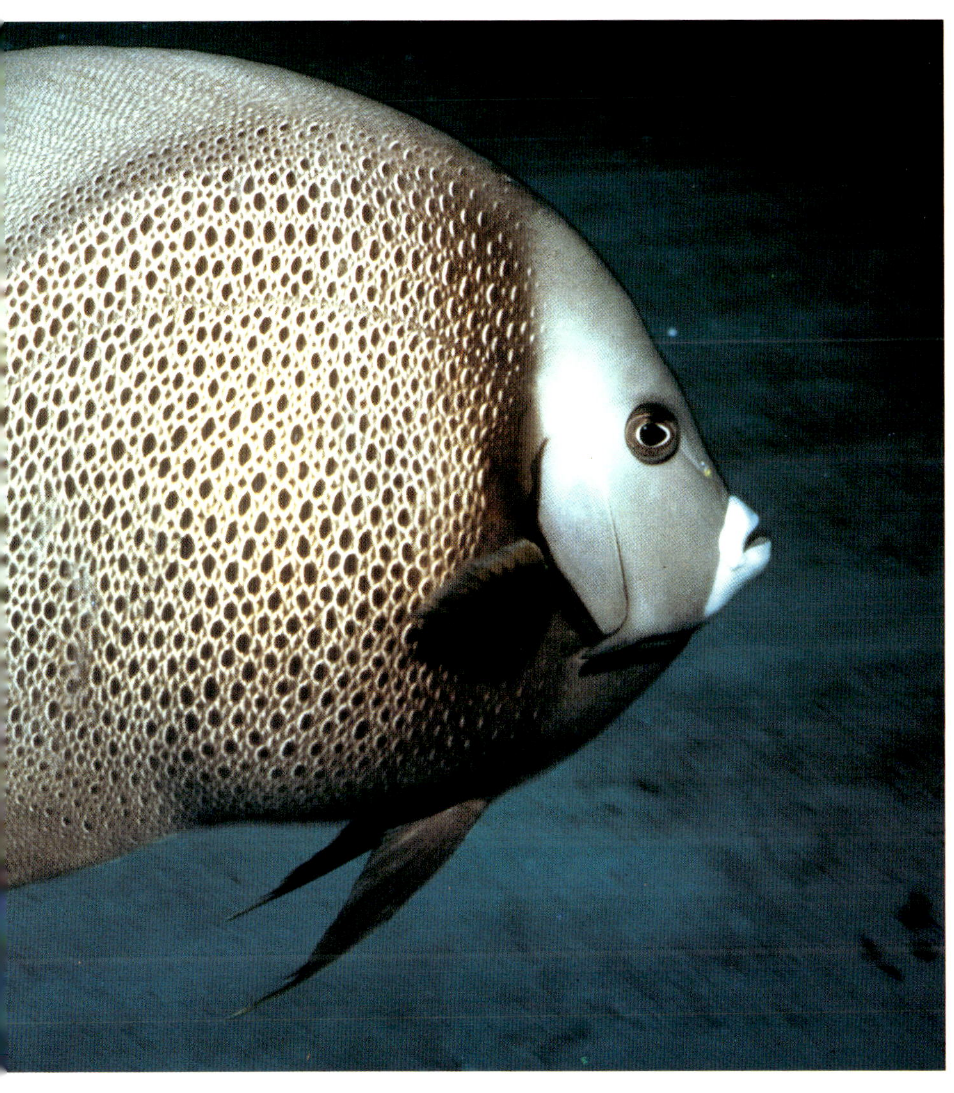

ABOVE: This is one of my very first underwater photographs, taken in 1980 with a very basic system: Nikonos III camera, 28mm lens, Nikonos SB-101 strobe, and Kodachrome 64 film. It illustrates the point that you don't need a fancy system of multiple camera bodies and lenses to get good underwater pictures. OPPOSITE TOP: The Sea & Sea SLR/housing system offers photographers shooting flexibility—under *and* above water. OPPOSITE MIDDLE: Sea & Sea's Seamaster Pro is perhaps one of the easiest-to-use underwater cameras on the market. OPPOSITE BOTTOM: The Nikonos RS is the world's first underwater autofocus 35mm SLR camera.

28mm, 20–35mm zoom, and 50mm macro. These lenses, labeled R-UW lenses, work only on the RS camera; standard Nikonos lenses fit only the Nikonos V system.

If you have recently purchased a Nikonos V, don't worry. Nikon has a strong commitment to its loyal Nikonos V owners and sees the Nikonos RS as the camera for those underwater shooters who want a camera on the cutting edge of technical sophistication.

You can pick up the complete Nikonos RS system for about $8,000.

Sea & Sea Seamaster Pro: Several features make the Seamaster Pro one of the easiest underwater cameras to use. This compact and lightweight 35mm camera features a built-in flash (optional flash units are available), TTL flash exposure (which measures the light entering the lens and turns off the flash when the correct amount of light has reached the film plane), underwater interchangeable lens capability, auto film advance, auto DX settings (which automatically set the film speed) for ISO 100 and 400 films, and auto film advance/power rewind. (ISO 100 film is recommended for topside shooting. Under water, you can use ISO 100 for close-ups and ISO 400 for wide-angle shooting. ISO 200 print film may deliver good results, too, because of the film's wide exposure latitude, which can produce good prints even if the negative is slightly over- or underexposed.)

Under water, interchangeable lens capability is a practical feature. For example, on a single dive you could take a portrait of a fellow diver with the camera's built-in 35mm lens, flip a switch for close-ups from three feet to eighteen inches, mount the 20mm or 16mm accessory lens on the camera to capture a seascape, and finally add a macro lens with a framer (a lens-mountable wire device in which you position the subject) for dramatic portraits of small reef creatures. Naturally, to use all these accessories a photographer would need an underwater assistant.

The Seamaster Pro sells for about $450.

For its Seamaster Pro, Sea & Sea offers several add-on strobes. For starters, there's the YS-50 TTL Flash Kit (about $300), which contains a YS-50 TTL flash (with cord), Sea Arm, and base plate (which allows the unit to be mounted on a camera). For more serious photographers who want to experiment with dual-, top-, side-, and backlighting, there's the Dual Flash Kit YS-50 TTL MMII (about $500), which is designed for use with the aforementioned flash kit. It includes one YS-50 TTL II flash, dual sync connector (so two strobes can be used), dual base plate, and Sea Arm.

Sea & Sea Pro accessories: Sea & Sea offers Nikonos V system owners a line of professional accessories that can expand the capability of the camera. Here's a look at just a few.

The Pro U/W YS-200 underwater strobe features two manual power settings (full and half power), a built-in slave (providing the capability to fire off-camera without the need for a sync cord), a quick-charge battery pack, and a 110-degree angle of coverage. A flexible ball-joint arm designed for the YS-200 enables photographers to position the strobe in precisely the right position for a desired lighting effect.

Sea & Sea also offers two TTL strobes for the Nikonos V. Both the YS-50 and new YS-300-N can be used on the Nikonos V system when the camera is set in the automatic, or "A," position.

For those sweeping underwater seascapes and full-frame pictures of divers, Sea & Sea offers three wide-angle lenses—12mm, 15mm, and 20mm—for the Nikonos V system. In addition, Sea & Sea offers a set of extension tubes for close-up photographs, enabling shooters to get 1:1 (life-size) magnifications of tiny reef critters.

Saving Money on Equipment (money that you then can spend on dive travel!)

Previously owned equipment is a good alternative to new gear, if you are 100 percent positive that it has never flooded—or that it has been repaired by a qualified repair person.

Helix, a Chicago, Illinois–based company that handles various photographic needs (and even has a special underwater photography department), has used equipment that sells for lots less than brand-new models. For $200 to $350, you can pick up a used Sea & Sea Motormarine II. Used Nikonos V systems are about $380 to $400 with a 35mm lens. (A new Nikonos V with a 35mm lens will sell for about $625, and a new Nikonos SB-103 strobe sells for about $425.)

Rental gear is another alternative. Renting is practical for cameraless divers who want to get their fins wet in underwater photography. Here are some ballpark prices for what's available on live-aboard vessels (prices are per day, from the Aggressor Fleet's listings):

❋ Nikonos V—$20;
❋ Nikonos SB-103 flash—$20;
❋ 15mm and 20mm lenses—$25;

❋ 28mm and 35mm lenses—$20;

❋ extension tubes—$5;

❋ photo package, consisting of a Nikonos V, Nikonos SB-103, 28mm or 35mm lens—$40 (or $175 for the whole charter);

❋ on-board processing—$10 per roll (Ektachrome and Fujichrome only, and no print films).

Most dive resorts in the Caribbean also have photo rental gear, and the prices are about the same.

Helix rents amateur (as well as professional) underwater equipment and will ship anywhere in the country. Helix's main number is 312-421-6000, and the switchboard can direct you to the rental department. Here are their approximate rental prices for popular underwater gear:

❋ Sea & Sea Motormarine I—$40 for one week ($10 each additional day);

❋ Nikonos V with 35mm lens—$60 for one week ($10 each additional day).

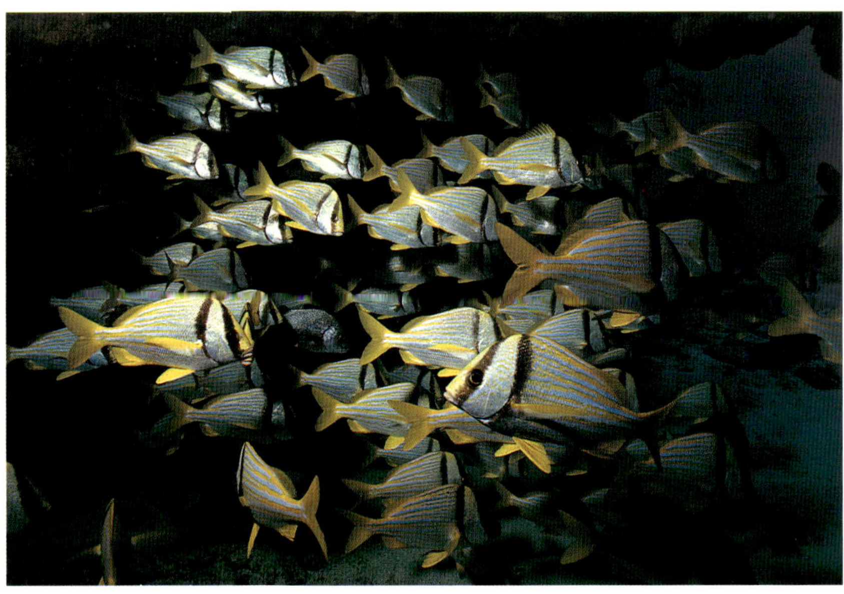

Dramatic close-ups are not always taken with close-up and macro lenses and dual strobe lighting. **Subject:** Porkfish. **Site:** Belize, Central America. **Equipment and film:** Nikonox V, Sea & Sea 15mm lens, YS-200 strobe, Kodachrome 64 film.

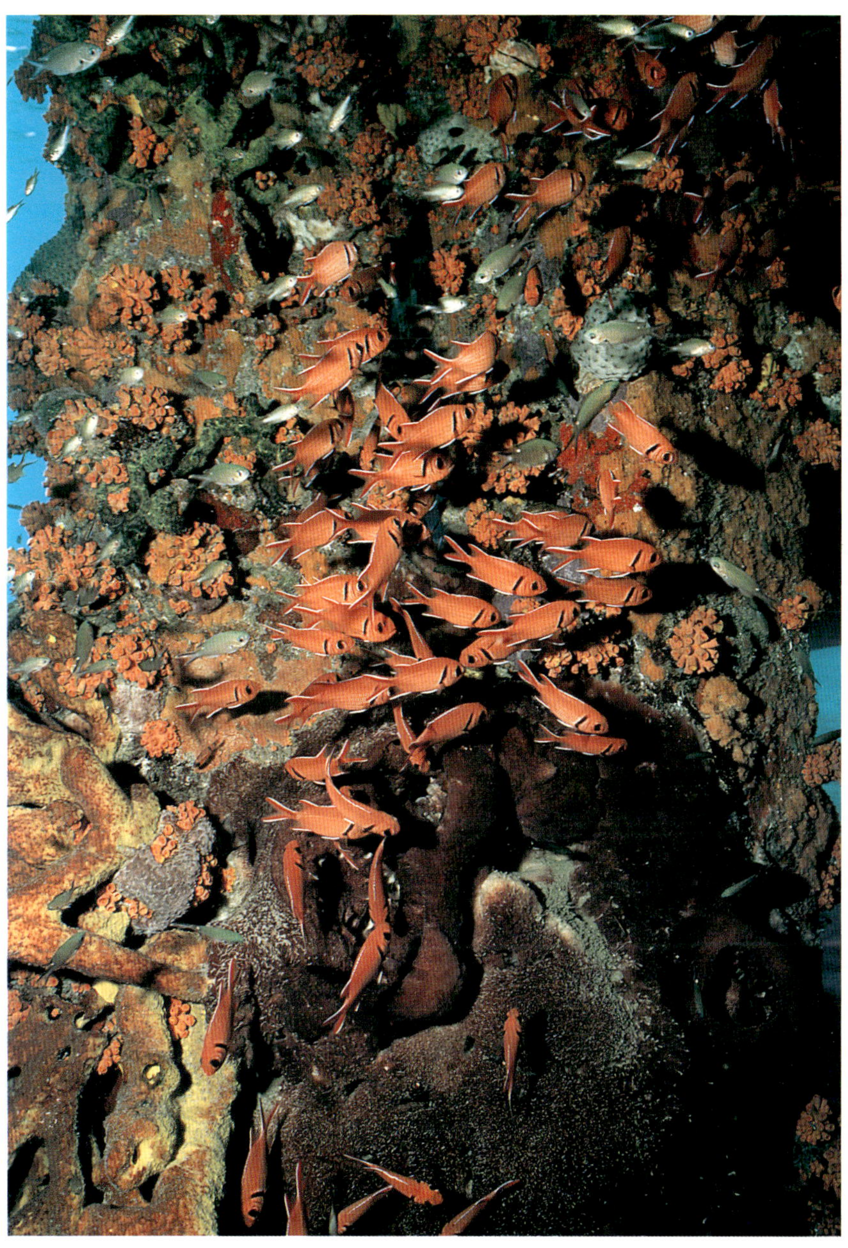

Composing wide-angle scenes is not as critical as composing macro photographs, so viewfinder cameras such as the Nikonos V or Sea & Sea Seamaster Pro can deliver near-perfect results—if you follow the correction marks in the finder when shooting close to your subject. **Subject:** Big eyes and sponge. **Site:** Bonaire Town Pier, Netherlands Antilles. **Equipment and film:** Sea & Sea Seamaster Pro, 20mm adapter lens, YS-50 strobe, Fujichrome 100.

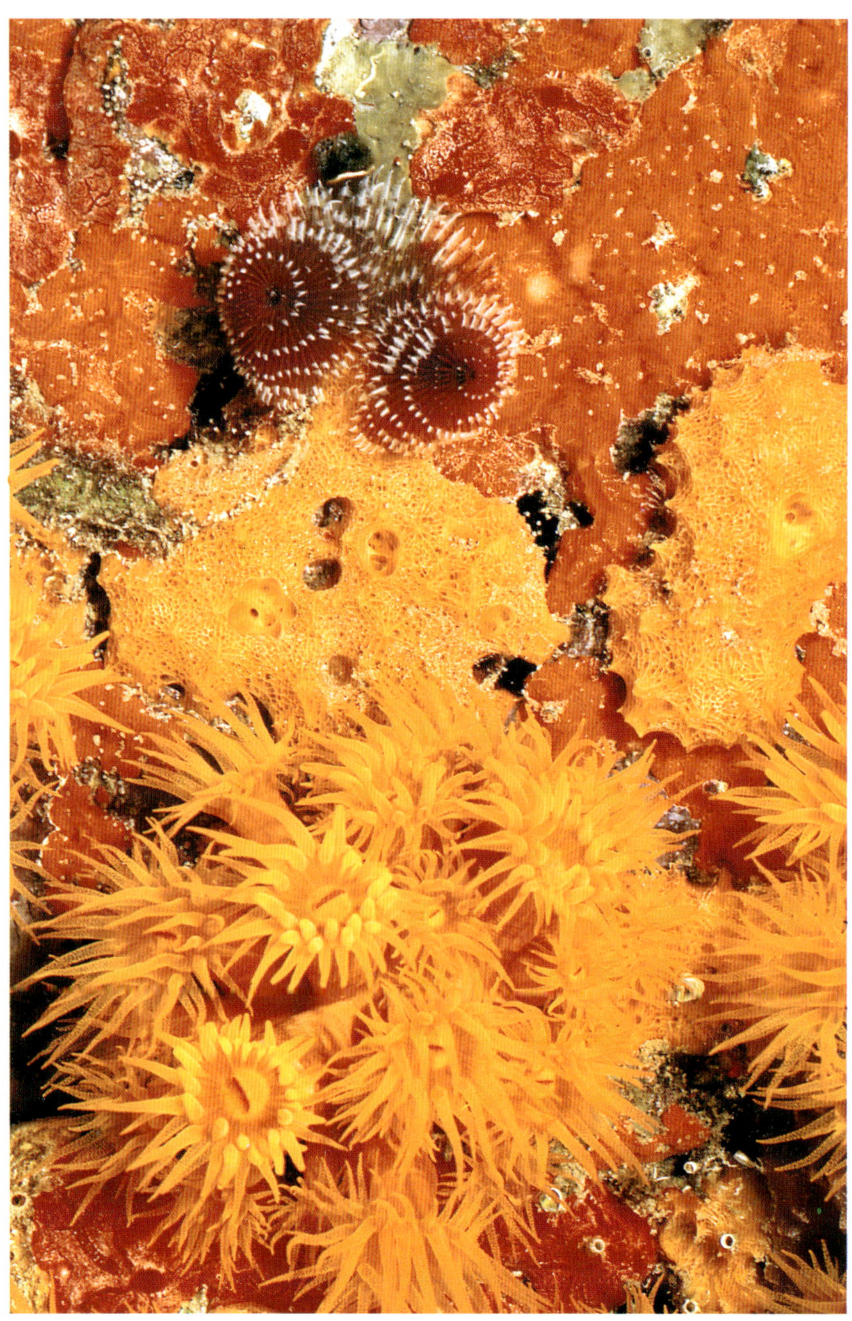

Few subjects on our planet offer as much color as the coral reef. To record this dramatic color, I usually use a very fine-grain film. **Subject:** Orange cup corals and Christmas tree worms. **Site:** Bonaire Town Pier, Netherlands Antilles. **Equipment and film:** Nikonos RS, 50mm lens, two Nikonos SB-103 strobes, Kodachrome 64.

Chapter 2: Choosing the Right Film

From print film to slide film to specialized underwater film—the advantages and disadvantages.

The underwater environment, bursting with color, is a photographer's paradise. To record these colors to your personal liking, pay special attention to your film choice.

You can choose from more than fifty different films for your underwater photography adventures. Each film has its own characteristics. Some are "warm"—tending to record colors as more red, orange, or yellow—while others are "cool"—tending toward blues and greens. Slow films have fine grain and fast films have larger grain. And some films offer brighter colors or more contrast than others.

Start simple. For your first few dives, I suggest that you try shooting with ISO 200 or 400 print film. Under water, fast print film offers three advantages. First, it lets you shoot at small f-stops, which offer good depth of field. In the underwater environment, where subjects are often moving or are at different distances from the camera, this is a big benefit. Second, the wide exposure latitude of print film gives you a better chance of getting a good exposure. Remember, your exposure must be "right on" with slide film. This can be a bit tricky under water, especially when photographing highly reflective fish next to divers with dark wet suits. Third, when shooting natural light pictures, a fast film allows a faster shutter speed than a slow film, so you have a better chance of "freezing" the action in your picture.

Once you become familiar with your underwater gear and the different underwater shooting conditions, you may want to switch to fine-grain slide film with an ISO rating of 50 or 64. As with above-water photography, fine-grain slide film is desirable for commercial purposes and when making enlargements.

The relatively new news in film for underwater photographers is Kodak's

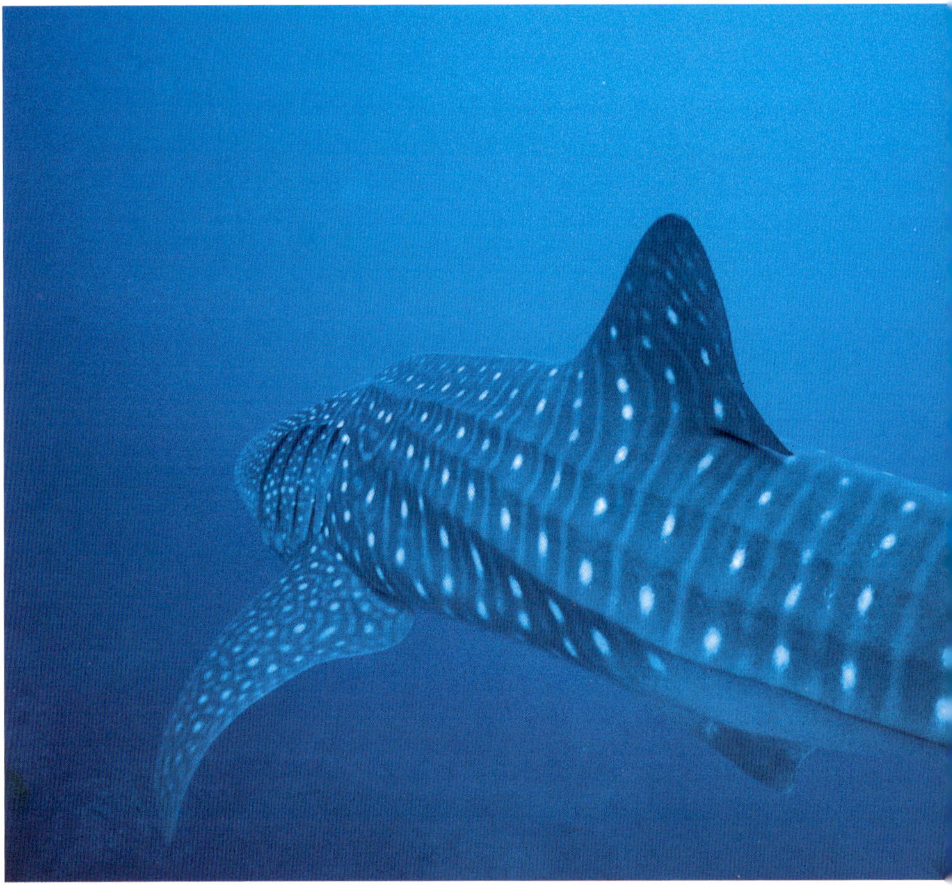

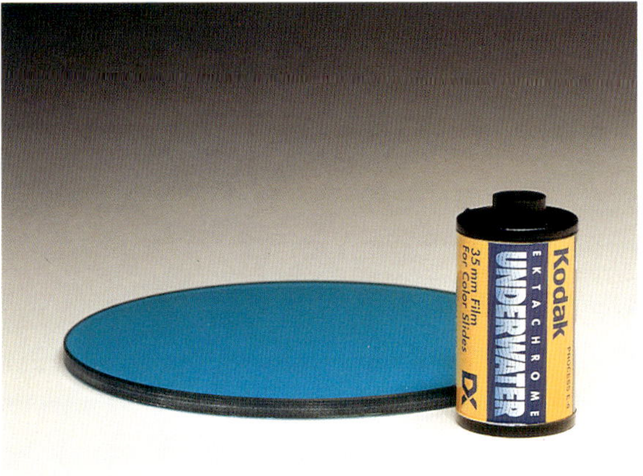

RIGHT: Ektachrome Underwater film by Kodak is designed specifically for taking pictures beneath the waves. When used with a Tiffen filter, Ektachrome Underwater can deliver excellent color in your pictures.

ABOVE: In low-light situations, a fast film may be required to photograph large subjects and large sections of a coral reef. Here, Kodachrome 200 was pushed to ISO 500, which provided a fast enough shutter speed to stop the action. The photo is a bit grainy, but a soft and grainy photo is better than no photo at all. **Subject:** Whale shark. **Site:** Galapagos Islands, Equador. **Equipment and film:** Nikonos V, 15mm lens, Kodachrome 200 pushed to ISO 500.

Ektachrome Underwater film, which is designed specifically for underwater use. It balances the red deficiency created by water-filtered light and is substantially more sensitive to red light than conventional daylight films. For underwater photographers, this is a tremendous advantage over standard 35mm film.

The Ektachrome Underwater film will deliver improved natural light color photographs at depths below ten feet and above forty feet (approximately). For flash pictures, you need to use one of two glass filters manufactured exclusively by Tiffen, called Tiffen filters: a Tiffen UW 0-2 when the subject is less than two feet away, or a Tiffen UW 2-7 when the subject is two to seven feet from the camera. These filters, which cover the strobe, are needed when taking flash pictures because the film is balanced for natural light—not the light from the flash. Without these filters, pictures will look more red. No filtration is needed for flash exposures beyond seven feet. In addition, the film is not recommended for ambient light exposures at depths of less than ten feet.

The thirty-six-exposure Kodak Ektachrome Underwater film is available in ISO 50, but can be pushed to ISO 100 for extra depth of field or a higher shutter speed. Pushing film is a technique in which you shoot photographs with your camera set at a film speed higher than the film's ISO number, and then have the film processed longer than normal to ensure proper exposure. (See also the section on color in "The Underwater Environment—A Photographer's View," and the section on wide-angle natural light pictures in "Capturing the Wide View—Naturally and with a Strobe.")

Once you find a film you like for a particular situation, such as macro, natural light, or flash conditions (and you may have to test several different brands and speeds before you find one that delivers the results you're looking for), it's advisable to stay with that one film for the particular situation. Remember, in underwater photography, you want as few variables as possible.

One final tip on film: Pack more than you think you'll need. If you are a first-time shooter, you'll probably over shoot, which is not surprising considering the beauty that awaits you under water. (See also "What to Bring on Your Dive Trip—Essential Accessories.")

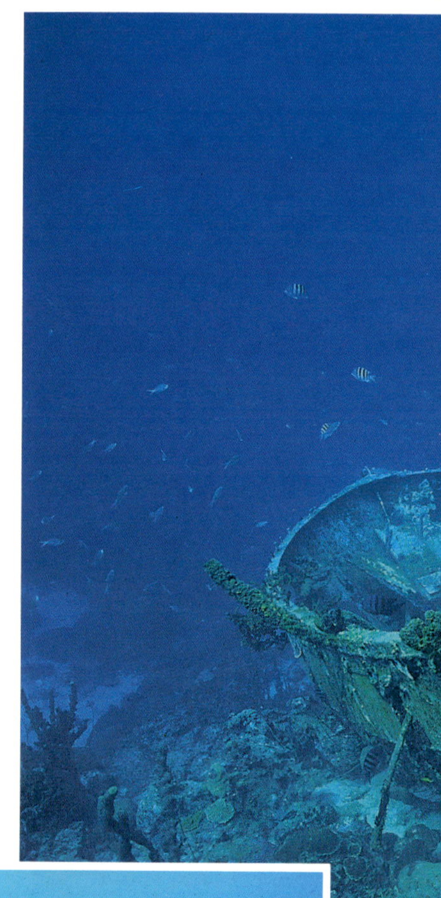

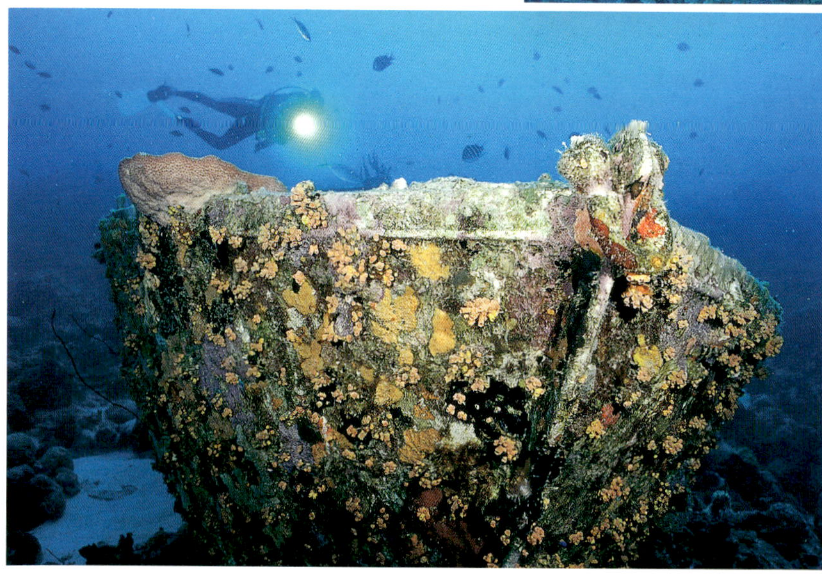

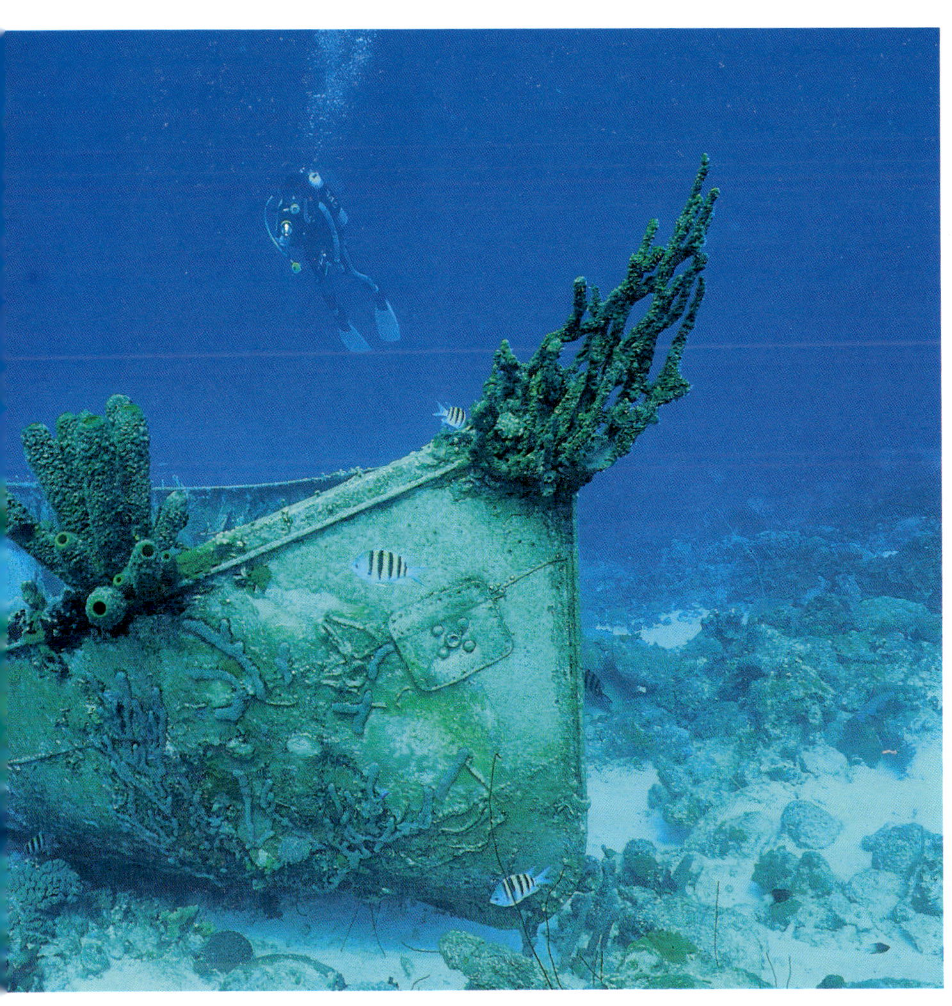

ABOVE: When planning a dive trip, it's a good idea to pack the types of film you will need for the different situations you expect. I always take faster film (ISO 200) to capture the natural look of underwater scenes, as illustrated above. OPPOSITE: I also take fine-grain film (ISO 100) to record the true color of subjects. **Subject:** Sunken rowboat. **Site:** Bonaire, Netherlands Antilles. **Equipment and film:** ABOVE: Nikonos V, 15mm lens, Ektachrome 200. OPPOSITE: Nikonos V, 15mm lens, Nikonos SB-104 strobe, Kodak Elite 100.

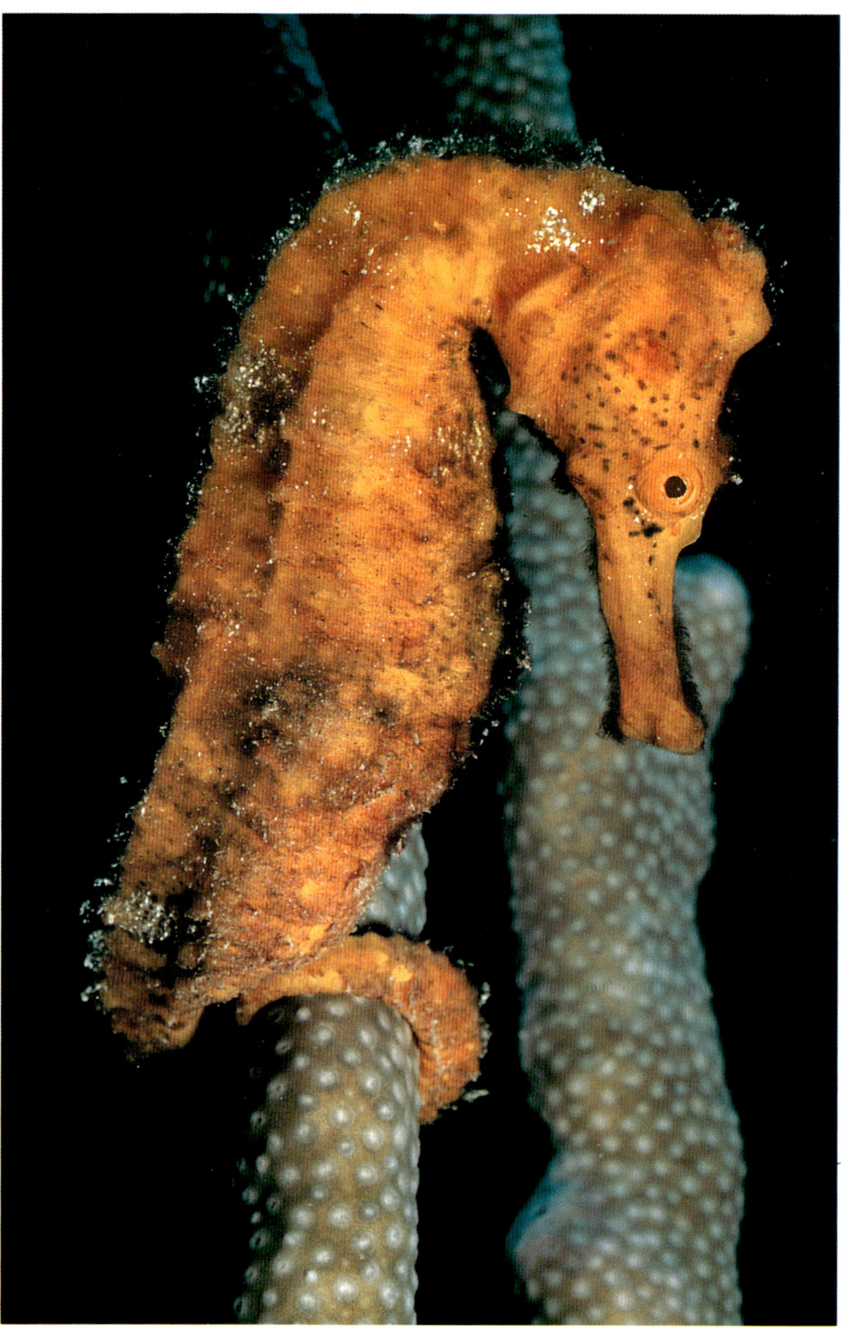

Fancy lighting equipment is not required for great underwater photographs. Here, a single strobe positioned over the lens—so the shadow fell behind the subject—was used. **Subject:** Sea horse. **Site:** Bonaire, Netherlands Antilles. **Equipment and film:** Nikonos RS, 50mm macro lens, Nikonos SB-104 strobe, Kodachrome 64.

Chapter 3: Selecting the Right Strobe

A strobe can be an essential tool for creativity and photo quality. How do you know which one is right for you?

An underwater strobe is both an invaluable accessory and a creative tool. It can bring out the true color of a subject, which may not be visible in natural light. In addition, adding artificial light to an underwater scene increases the apparent sharpness and contrast of a picture.

Choosing the right strobe is *very* important. You don't want a strobe that is too big and bulky for you, yet you don't want one that won't deliver the kind of power you are looking for. In addition, strobes can cost as much as a camera—and even more. So you need to choose a strobe wisely so you have some money left over for your dive vacation.

Here's a quick look at some of the key features of underwater strobes and their benefits.

Strobe exposure modes: Most underwater strobes offer both automatic, or through-the-lens (TTL), and full-manual exposure control. More expensive models offer these features plus the option to control the manual light output by one-half, one-quarter, and one-sixteenth power. Top-of-the line units may also feature "slave" operation—the capability to fire off-camera without the need for a sync cord. If you are serious about underwater photography, having as many options as possible will give you maximum versatility and creative control.

Angle-of-coverage: The angle-of-coverage is the angle over which the strobe will deliver uniform illumination. If you want to light a full-frame image, you'll need a strobe that covers the angle-of-view of the widest lens you plan to use with your flash. Flash coverage information is included in the literature that comes with each strobe. Read it carefully before you buy.

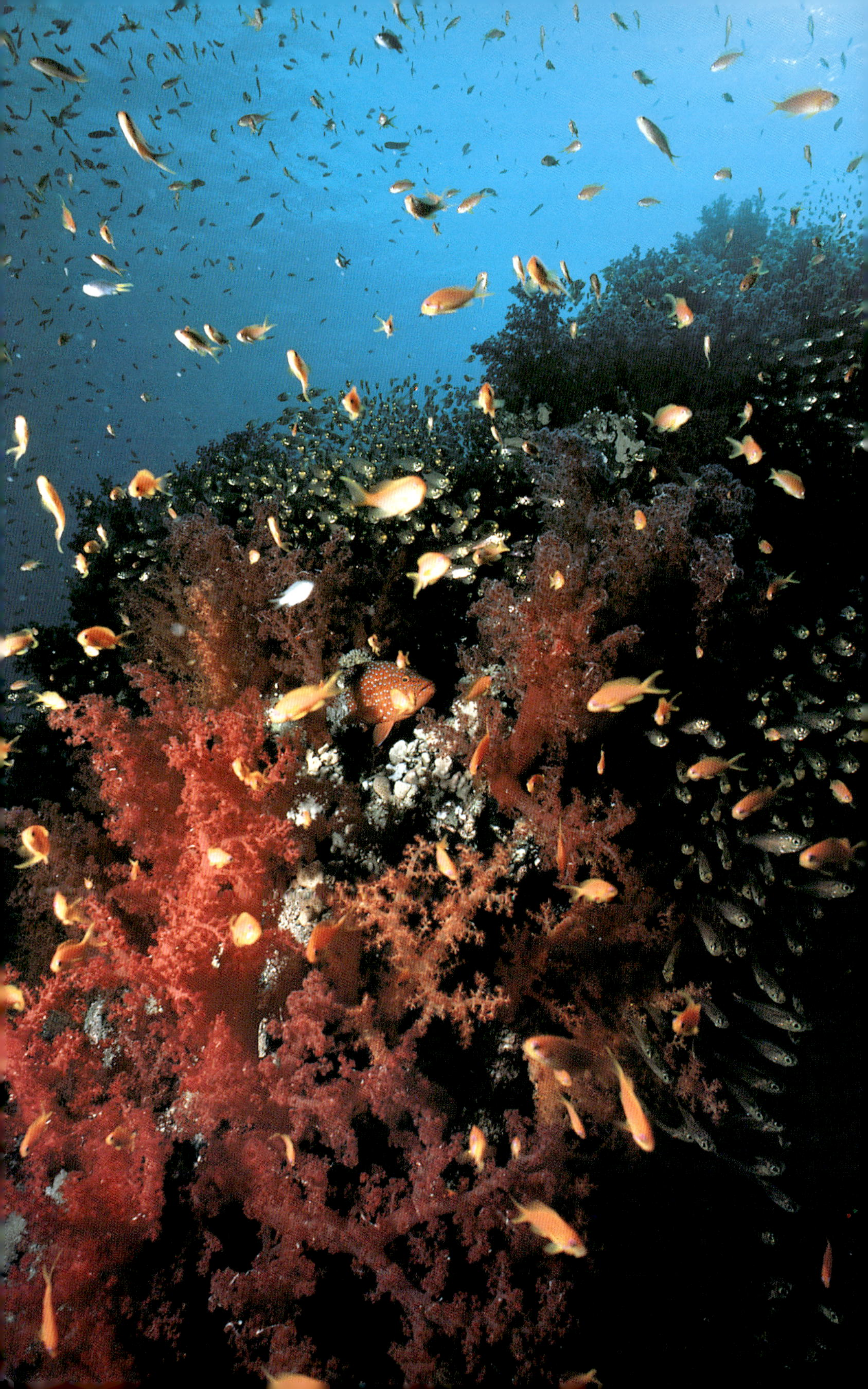

You don't want to end up with a strobe that covers only a 28mm lens if you want to shoot with a 15mm or wider lens.

Basically, most strobes offer at least 35mm shooting capability, either with wide-beam reflectors or via supplied diffusers. There are exceptions, however, so this point should not be overlooked when shopping for a strobe.

Battery power: Battery power for strobes comes in various forms. If you buy a unit with a built-in, rechargeable nickel-cadmium (nicad) battery, you'll have to depend on recharging capabilities at your dive site, either on a live-aboard boat or at your hotel. If you're traveling to the East Coast of Africa or other remote locations with unreliable electrical power, this may be a problem. In addition, if you do go with a nicad unit, pack a voltage converter along with your strobe.

Most strobes, however, use replaceable batteries, either AA, C, or D cells. The advantage to using these strobes is that you can take along all the batteries you need for a trip. The disadvantages are that a week's worth of batteries is fairly heavy, and disposing of batteries is a problem for the environment.

Modeling light for aiming: Accurately aiming a strobe underwater can be a challenge because subjects appear closer than they actually are (due to refraction), not to mention the fact that often they, like the photographer, are moving. A built-in modeling light helps you aim the strobe quickly and easily, especially on night dives. Attaching a small underwater flashlight to the strobe head with a rubber holster also works well. (See also "Shooting in the Dark.")

When choosing a strobe, make sure that the angle-of-coverage is at least equal to the angle-of-view of your widest lens. If it's smaller, your strobe will not fully light reef scenes. **Subject:** Soft corals. **Site:** Ras Mohammed, Red Sea. **Equipment and film:** Nikonos V, 15mm lens, Sea & Sea YS-200, Kodachrome 64.

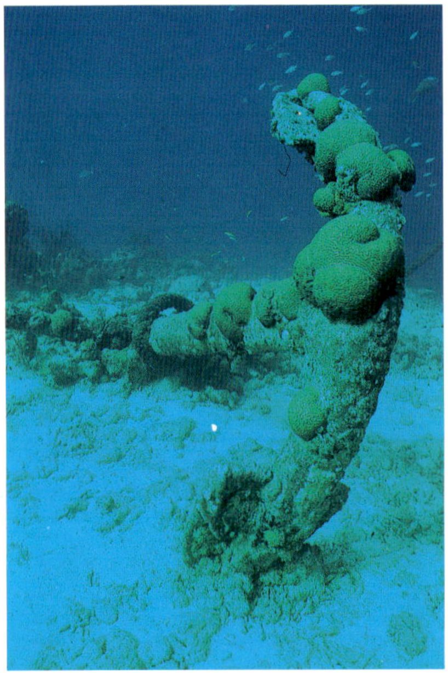 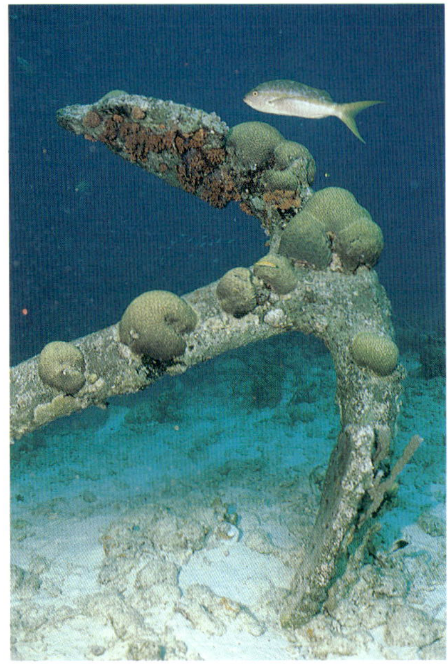

Usually, adding strobe light to underwater scenes can enhance a picture. However, there are exceptions, as illustrated in this series. The first photo (ABOVE LEFT) was taken in natural light. The next (ABOVE RIGHT) photograph was taken with a strobe, but light from the strobe reflecting off particles in the water created backscatter, ruining the picture. When the water column is filled with lots of particles, silhouettes can be effective, as illustrated (OPPOSITE TOP). The last photo (OPPOSITE BOTTOM) was taken on a different day, when visibility had improved. **Subject:** Divi Flamingo Beach Anchor. **Site:** Bonaire, Netherlands Antilles. **Equipment and film:** Nikonos RS, 20–35mm zoom lens set at 20mm, Nikonos SB-104 strobe, Kodak Elite 100.

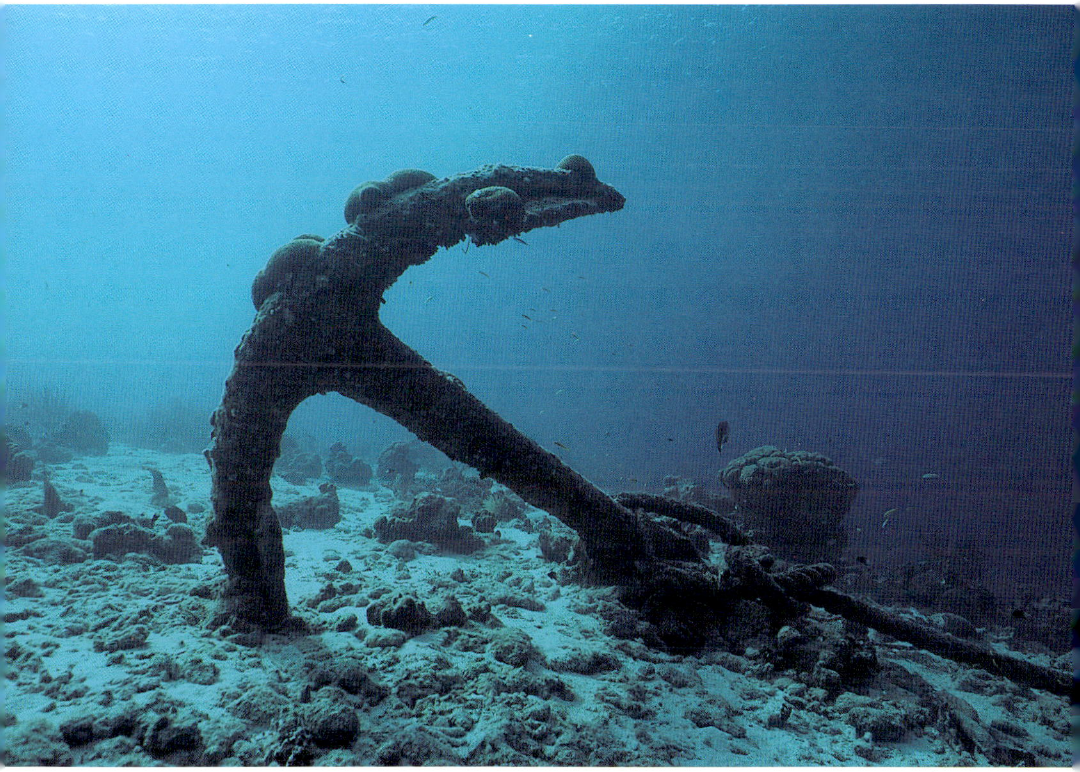

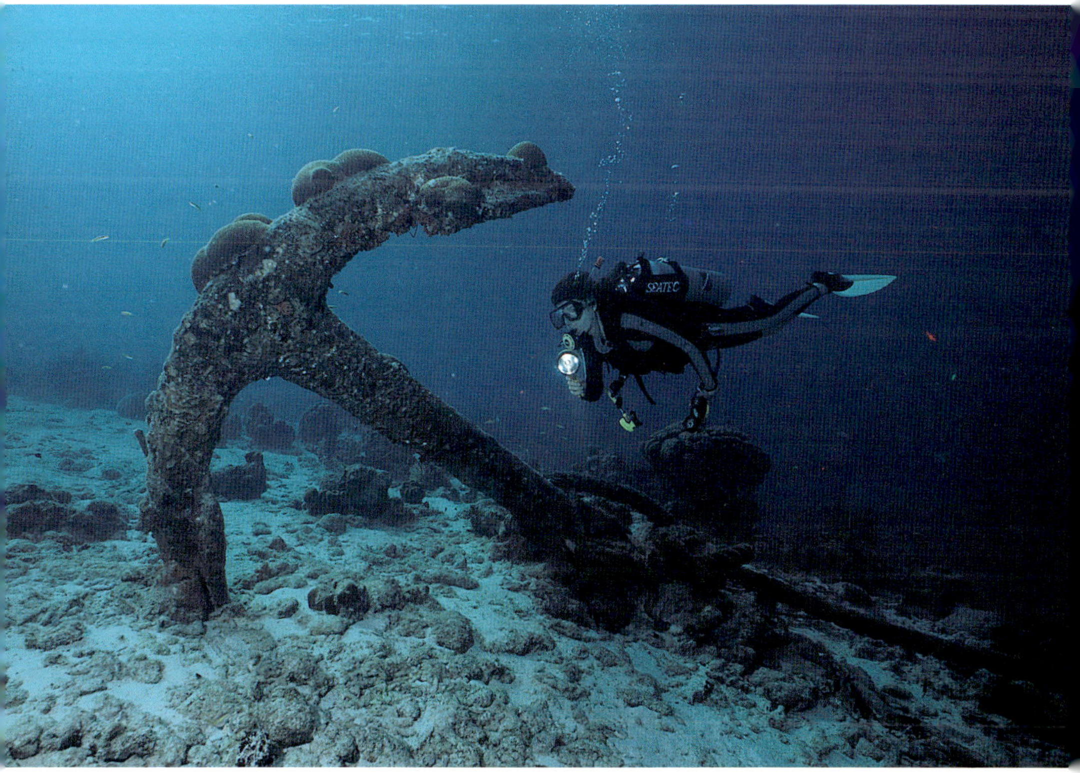

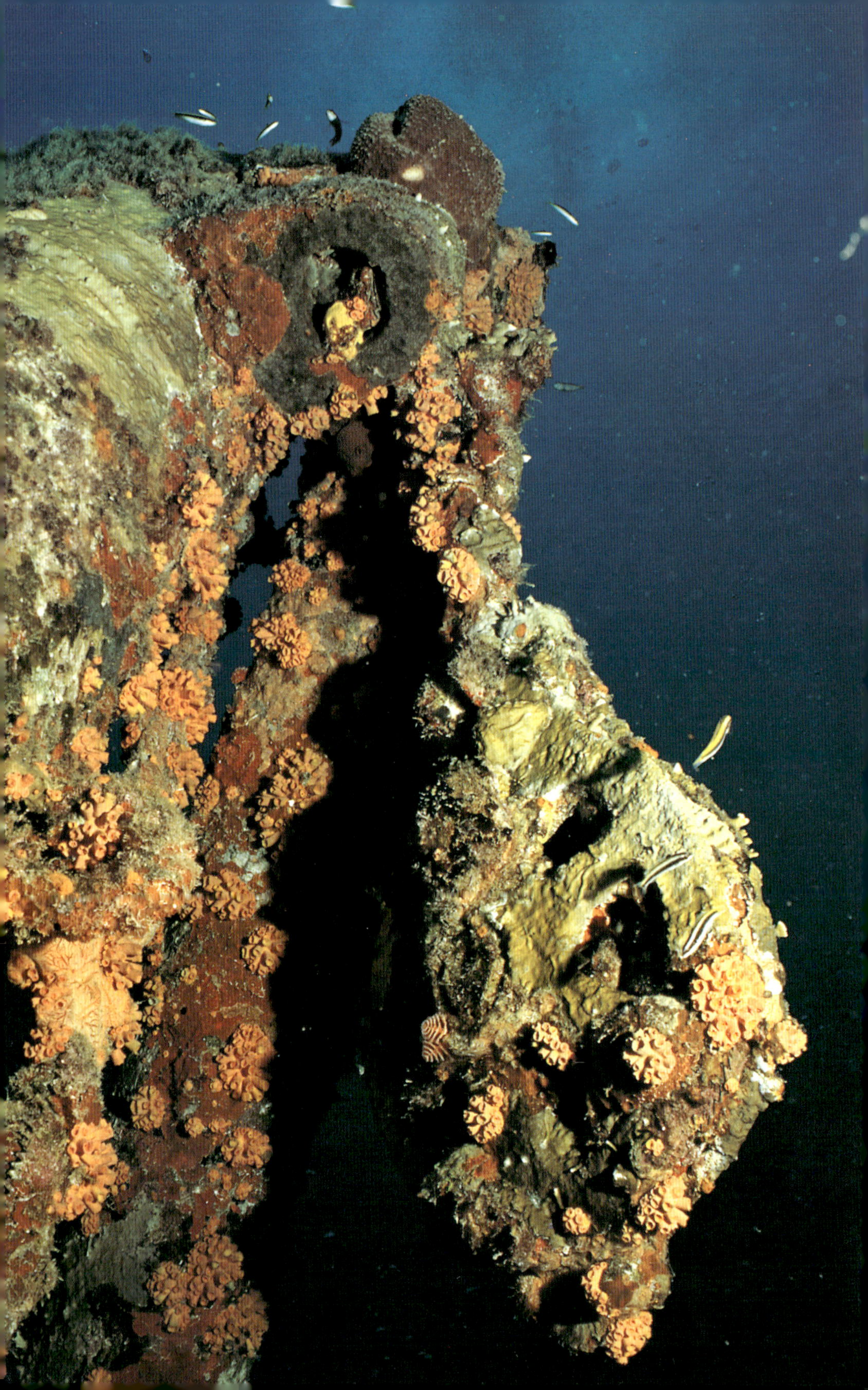

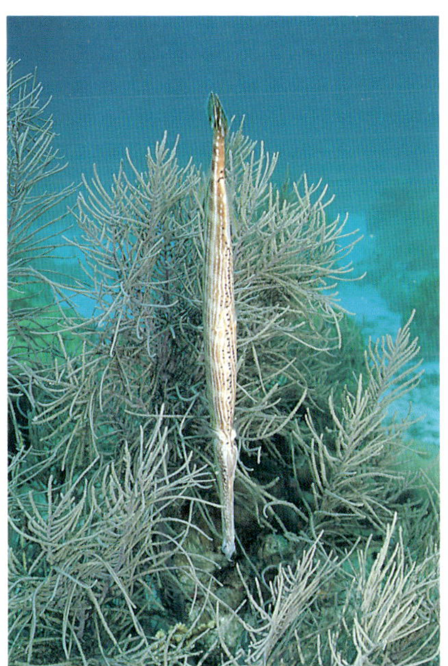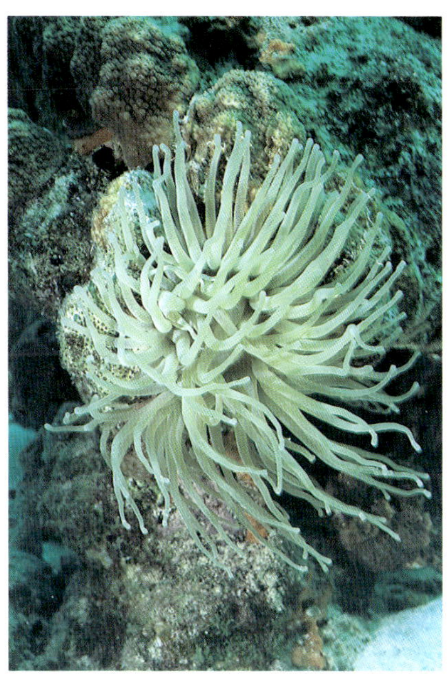

ABOVE: To get a natural-looking underwater strobe picture, the light from your strobe should be balanced to the natural light so your picture does not look like it was taken with a strobe. This is easy to accomplish with the Nikonos RS, which does the calculations for you. When shooting with a Nikonos V, adjust the *f*-stop so the shutter speed is 1/90 second, the flash sync speed. At this setting, the light from the flash will be evenly balanced to the natural light, if you are not beyond an acceptable flash-to-subject distance. **Subject:** (ABOVE LEFT): Trumpetfish in soft corals. (ABOVE RIGHT): Anemone. **Site:** Bonaire, Netherlands Antilles. **Equipment and film:** Nikonos RS, 50mm lens, Nikonos SB-104 strobe, Kodachrome 64.

OPPOSITE: If aimed correctly, one flash can evenly illuminate a subject. To aim my flash, I mount an underwater dive light on my strobe so I can see exactly where the strobe is aimed. In this example, the strobe was aimed in the middle of the picture. **Subject:** *Helma Hooker* wreck. **Site:** Bonaire, Netherlands Antilles. **Equipment and film:** Nikonos RS, 20–35mm zoom lens set at 20mm, Nikonos SB-104 strobe, Kodachrome 64.

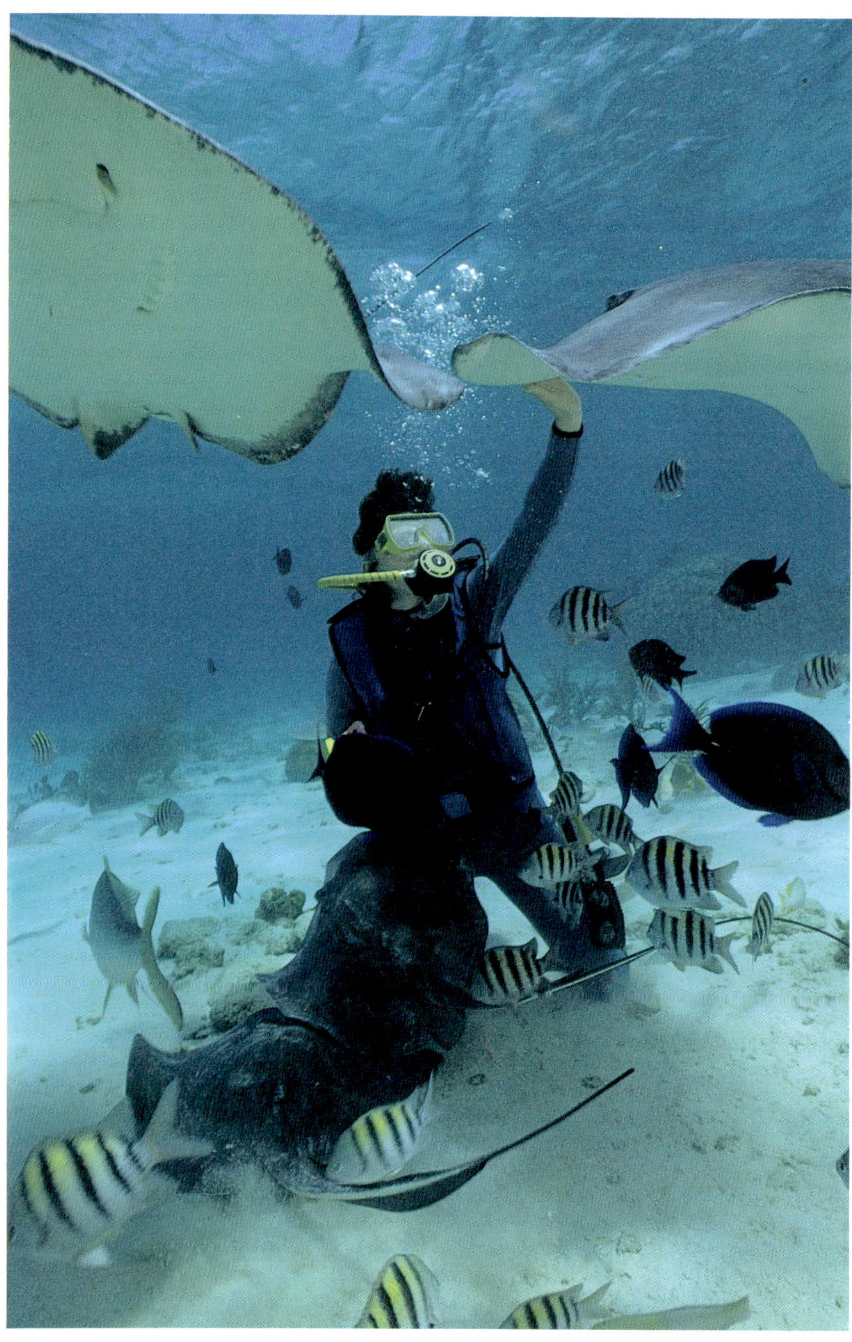

Many divers feel the best twelve-foot day dive in the world is at Stingray City, Grand Cayman. Situations like this—shallow, clear, and bright—offer good natural light photo opportunities. **Equipment and film:** Nikonos V, 15mm lens, Ektachrome Underwater.

Chapter 4: Where to Go for Great Pictures

Destinations that offer amazing subjects, from the Red Sea to the Florida Keys, the Cayman Islands to Fiji, and beyond.

If you want to get great pictures, you most certainly need photo know-how, the right equipment, and some luck. But there is another key ingredient for good underwater photographs: good subjects.

Good subjects can be found in just about any ocean. However, it often takes a skilled boat captain to take you to the most pristine reefs in an area for wide-angle photography, as well as to sites for interesting macro subjects. For this reason, I often dive from live-aboard vessels operated by the Aggressor Fleet, which runs charters to places like Honduras, Belize, Cayman Islands, Galapagos Islands, Hawaiian Islands, Costa Rica, Palau, Truk Lagoon in Micronesia, and the Turks and Caicos. The Aggressor captains know the reefs in these areas like the backs of their hands, so you don't waste any time getting to and from the best dive sites.

Aggressor ships are specifically designed for scuba diving and cater to the needs of underwater photographers, both beginners and professionals. Slide film processing is offered on board, so you can see which techniques work best for you and which ones don't—and come home with some great shots even on your first dive vacation. Photographic gear, including additional lenses, is available to rent. You can even take underwater photography courses during week-long cruises on these floating mini-hotels.

I recommend the Aggressor ships to underwater photographers for another reason: diver safety. Each ship has skilled dive masters and dive guides who watch over their passengers with tender loving care. This is important, because underwater photographers tend to focus all of their attention on getting those "once-in-a-lifetime" pictures and sometimes forget about safety. Having a "guardian angel dive guide" watching over you makes the whole experience that much more enjoyable.

For more information on the Aggressor Fleet, call the Aggressor office at 800-348-2628, or write Aggressor Fleet, PO Drawer K, Morgan City, LA 70381.

Here's a quick look at what you'll encounter beneath the waves at just a few of my favorite "underwater photo studios."

Belize: The Belize Barrier Reef, off the cost of Belize in Central America, is the second-largest coral reef in the world. Lots of shallow, soft coral gardens are found here along with plenty of Caribbean fishes—especially on the off-shore atolls of Glovers Reef and Lighthouse Reef. A popular dive site is the "Blue Hole," a huge hole in the reef that offers clear diving to 160 feet along sheer vertical walls. The view is spectacular, so bring your 15mm lens, but you won't see many fishes here.

Cayman Islands: This tropical Caribbean paradise is only 190 miles south of Cuba. In the Caymans, the two most dived islands are Grand Cayman and Little Cayman. Grand Cayman's most popular dive site is Sting Ray City, where dozens of tame sting rays frolic around divers in twelve feet of clear water. To capture these animals on film, I recommend a 15mm or 20mm lens. Shoot on automatic in natural light with Ektachrome Underwater film and you should get good results. Little Cayman offers one of the best dives in the Caribbean: Bloody Bay Wall, a near-vertical coral wall with lush coral formations and lots of fishes. "Macro heaven" would be a good description of this area.

Cocos Island and Galapagos Islands: Both of these Pacific island chains offer ideal conditions for drift diving. Cocos Island is a well-worth-it, thirty-two-hour boat ride from the west coast of Costa Rica, and the Galapagos Islands are west of Equador. Drift divers are dropped off and a chase boat follows their bubbles as they explore the reef. The relatively strong currents carry lots of plankton, which in turn attract subjects like manta rays, whale sharks, and large schools of pelagic fish (which are fun to photograph with a wide-angle lens such as a 15mm). In the Galapagos, you'll also encounter play-ful sea lions on just about every dive! To take pictures in these waters, you need to be prepared to think fast because you are almost always on the move.

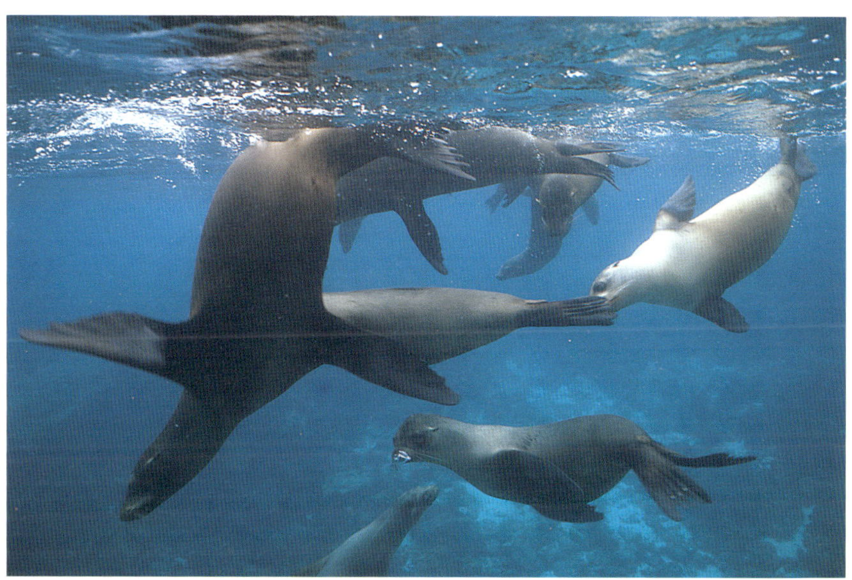

ABOVE: Great photo opportunities start a few feet below the surface in many dive locations. **Subject:** Sea lions. **Site:** Galapagos Islands, Ecuador. **Equipment and film:** Nikonos V, 15mm lens, Kodachrome 200 film. RIGHT TOP: Aggressor Fleet live-aboard vessels are based in some of the top dive destinations around the world. RIGHT MIDDLE: The key to getting good natural light pictures is to dive shallow (above thirty feet) and to use Kodak's Ektachrome Underwater film, which is designed for underwater use. **Subject:** Diver on coral-cover mast of shipwreck. **Site:** Truk Lagoon. **Equipment:** Nikonos V, Sea & Sea 15mm lens. RIGHT BOTTOM: Close-up photography does not necessarily mean using a close-up attachment or macro lens. Wide-angle lenses produce dramatic close-ups, too. Plus, they offer great depth-of-field. **Subject:** Spanish dancer egg case. **Site:** Kenya Coast. **Equipment and film:** Nikonos V, 15mm lens, Sea & Sea YS-200 strobe, Kodachrome 64 film.

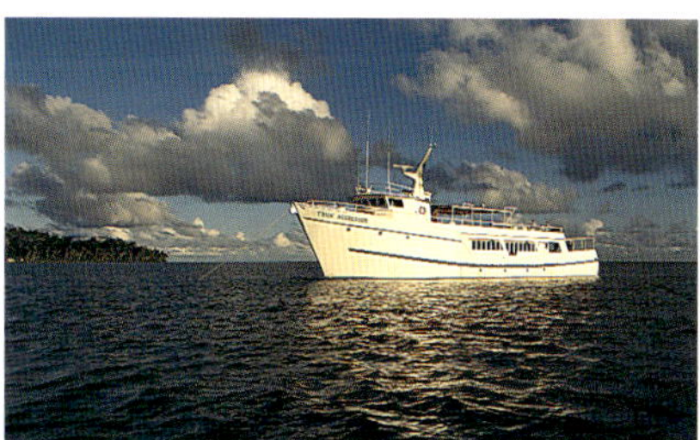

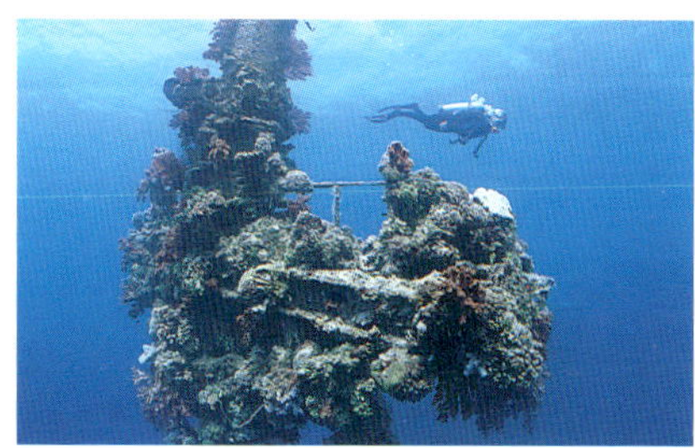

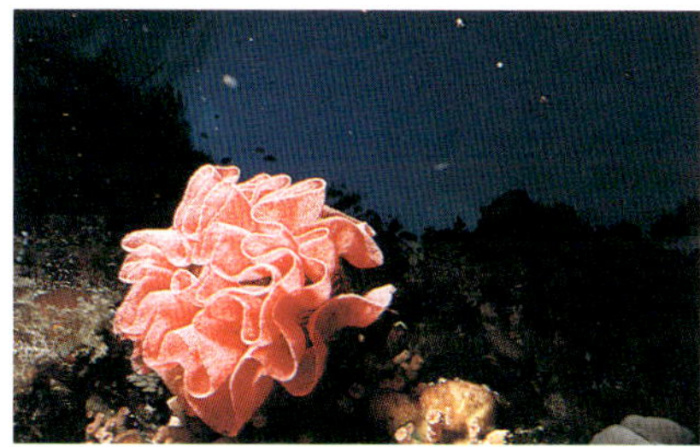

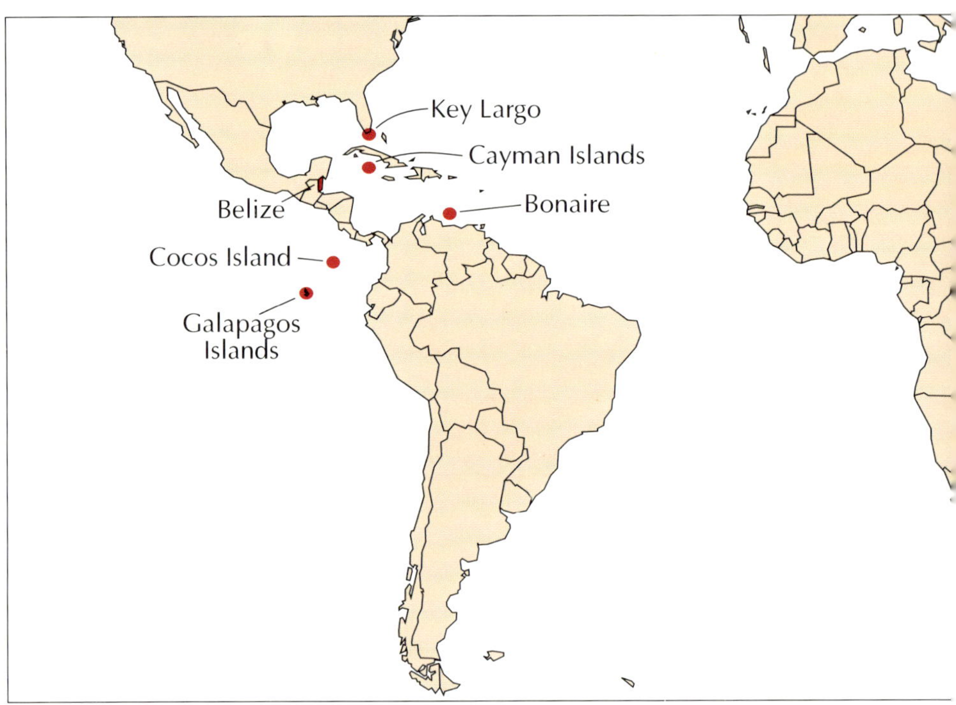

Palau: This chain of islands located about eight hundred miles off the southern tip of the Philippines is called Belau by the people who live there. What I like most about diving in Palau is the diversity of diving: shallow and deep-water reefs, all thriving with life; cave and cavern diving; and marine (saltwater) lakes filled with thousands of harmless jellyfish. Some marine biologists call Palau the "cradle of diversity" because these islands offer perhaps the greatest variety of marine life in the world. Underwater photographers can put all their lenses to use in these beautifully clear waters.

Truk Islands: At Truk Lagoon, in the Caroline Islands of Micronesia, sixty Japanese ships were sent to their graves in 1944 by U.S. war planes. The ships' hulls offer great wide-angle picture possibilities. In addition, the wrecks have become magnets for a wide variety of tropical fishes, including lionfish and clownfish, plus lush soft coral colonies. Therefore, night diving offers endless macro possibilities.

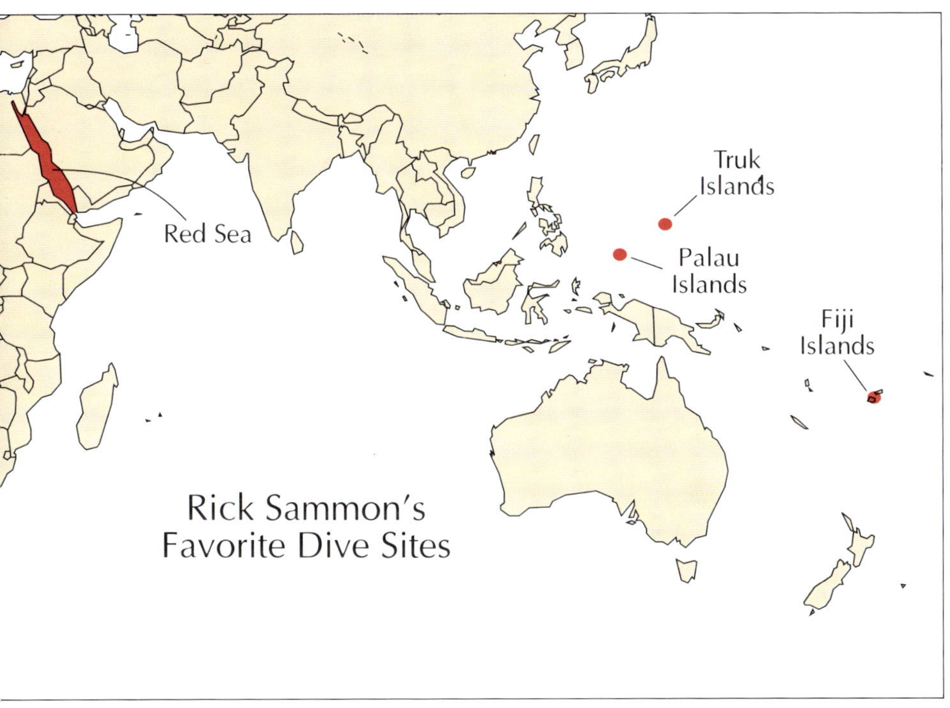

More great locations

When I'm not on an Aggressor live-aboard, I'm usually at one of the following sites. These, too, offer beginner and professional underwater photographers endless photo opportunities.

Bonaire: Bonaire is located in the Netherlands Antilles, off the coast of Venezuela in South America. The diving here is perhaps the easiest in the Caribbean because all major shore and boat dive sites are located on the lee (calm) side of the island. In fact, Bonaire nearly guarantees good shore diving 365 days a year and twenty-four hours a day. Perhaps the most spectacular macro dive site in the Caribbean is located in Bonaire, at the Bonaire Town Pier. Here, on dozens of pilings, live hundreds of colorful and exotic fishes and invertebrates.

While in Bonaire, I stay at the Divi Flamingo Resort, which offers underwater photo courses, equipment rental, and film processing. You can book your room and diving through the Divi's Florida office: 800-367-3484.

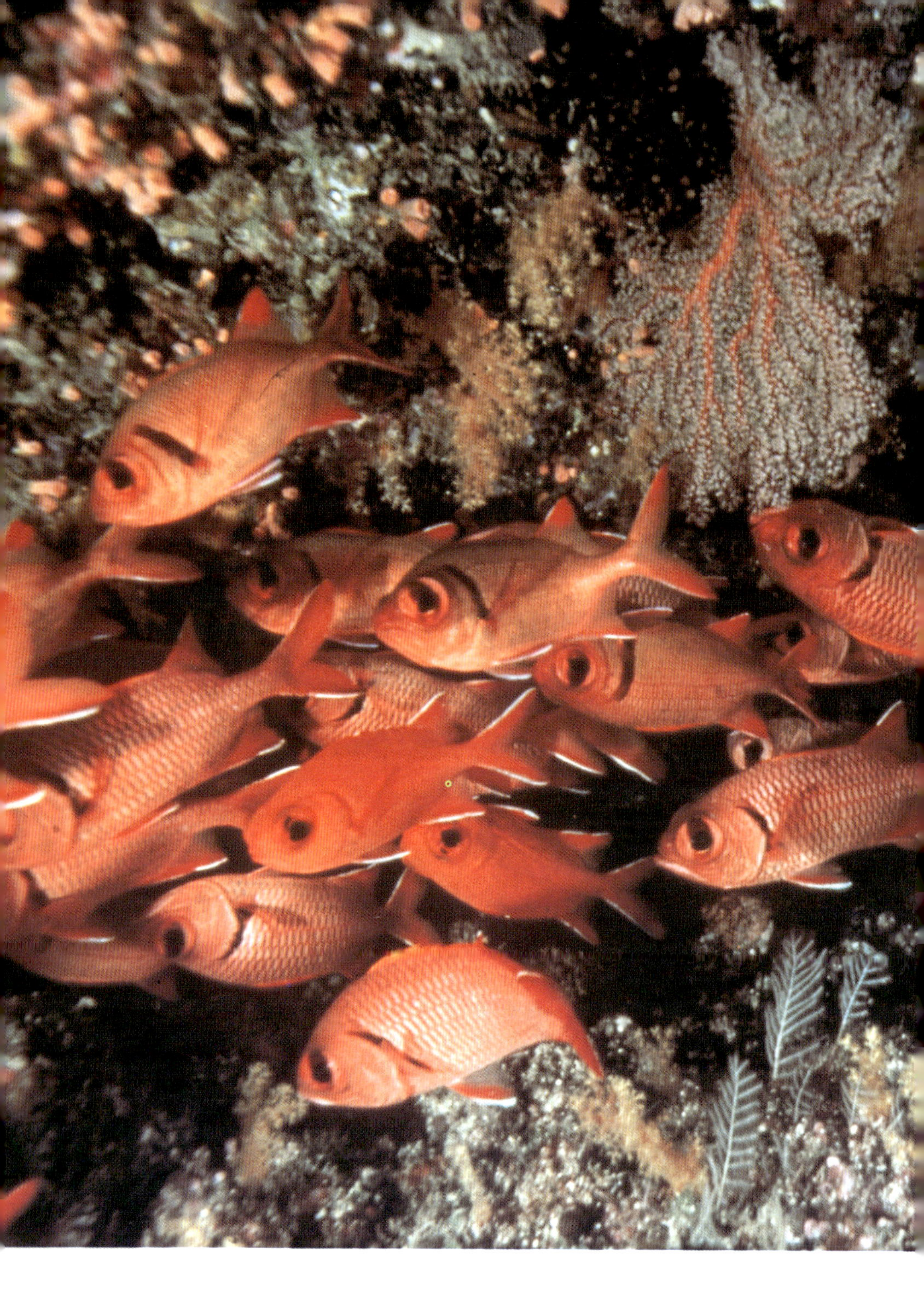

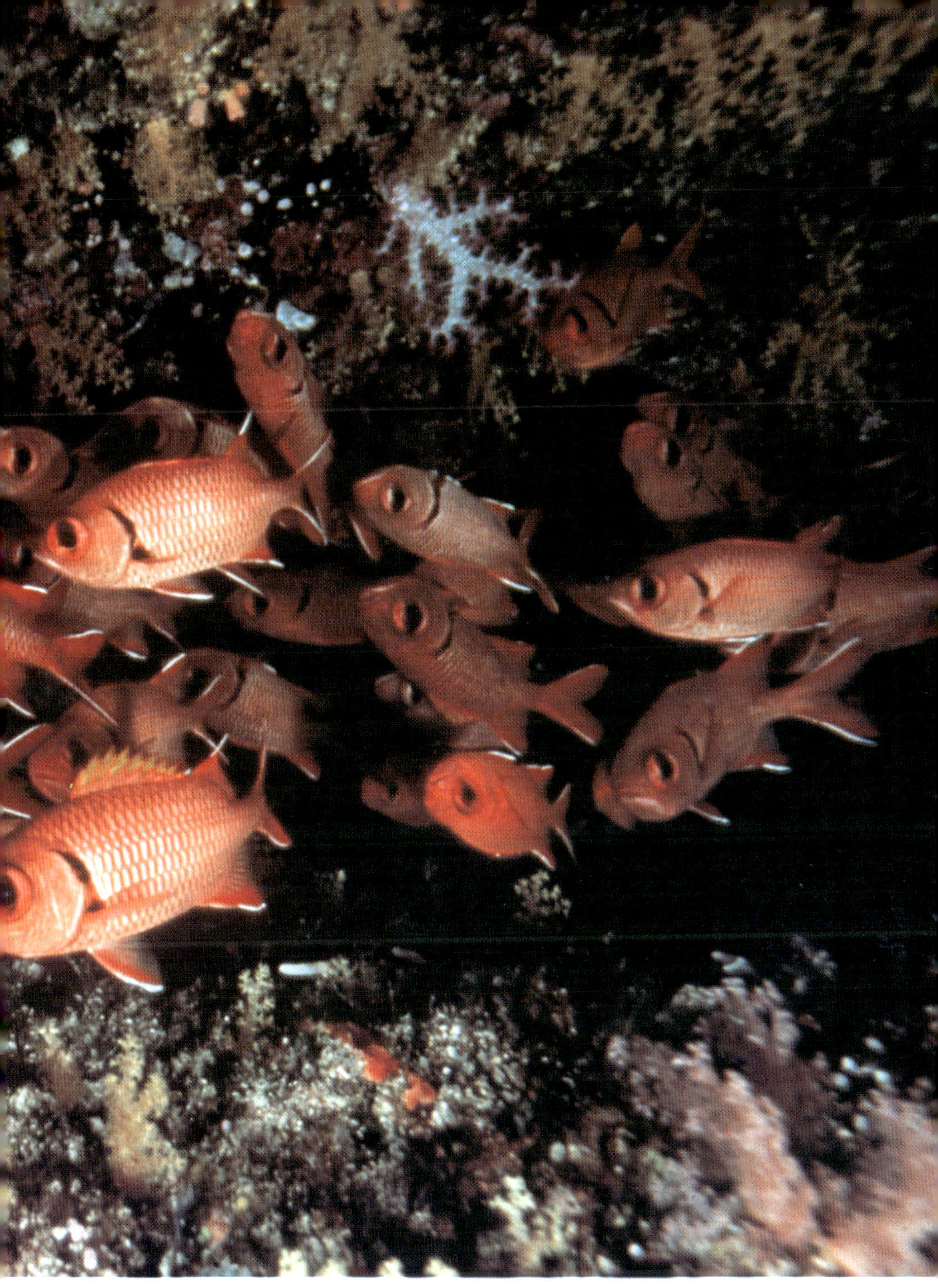

The nooks, crannies, and caves of the reef are filled with colorful subjects—but you must use an underwater strobe to record the true colors of the critters on film. **Site:** Palau. **Subject:** Big eyes in cave. **Equipment:** Stromm One underwater housing, Nikonos 8008, 20mm lens, two Nikonos SB-103 strobes, Kodachrome 64 film.

Key Largo: Closer to home, Key Largo in Florida (one hour south of Miami) offers shallow water (thirty to forty feet) and relatively easy diving. The reefs here don't offer as much color and fish life as the southern Caribbean reefs, but this is a good place for beginners to learn underwater photography. You can practice your shipwreck photography on several wrecks, wide-angle techniques on the reefs, and macro photography on sleeping fishes at night. Note, however, that the boat ride to the reefs takes about forty-five minutes, and it can get rough at times, especially from January to April.

There are dozens of dive shops and hotels in Key Largo. I usually dive with Captain Slate's Atlantis Dive Center: 800-331-DIVE.

Fiji: For me, Fiji is a magical place. North of New Zealand in the Pacific Ocean, this underwater environment is bursting with color. Soft corals seem to come in every color—red, yellow, green, purple, orange, and even white. If it's color you are after, you can't go wrong in Fiji. But don't get overwhelmed by the lush coral gardens; take a closer look and you'll find hundreds of macro subjects. Also, manta rays are frequently seen in these waters, so be prepared to capture these creatures on film with your wide-angle lens.

Red Sea: One of my favorite dive sites, the Red Sea in the Middle East offers just about everything for the underwater photographer: large schools of fish, lots of little reef goldfish hovering over coral heads, spectacular soft coral formations, and more macro subjects than you can photograph in a week's time. In addition, the visibility in the Red Sea is often over one hundred feet. My favorite dives are at Ras Mohammed, Anemone City, and The Temple.

Diving charters to Fiji and the Red Sea can be organized by See & Sea Travel, 50 Francisco Street, San Francisco, CA 94113. Or call 800-DIV-XPRT (800-348-9778).

Wherever you go on your underwater adventures, planning is the final

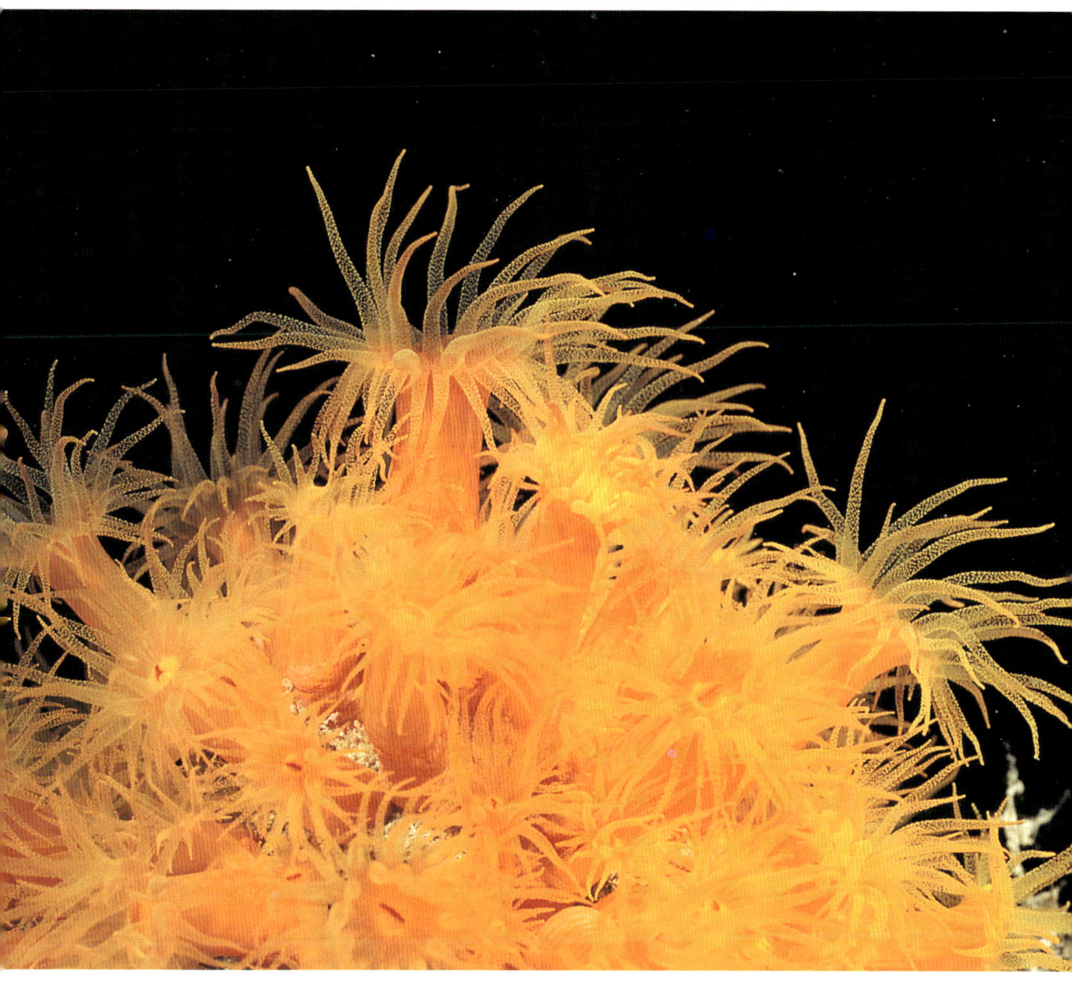

If you want sharp and colorful underwater pictures, follow this rule: Shoot close.
Site: Bonaire Town Pier, Netherlands Antilles. **Subject:** Orange cup corals.
Equipment and film: Stromm One Underwater housing, Nikon 8008, 60mm lens, two Nikonos SB-103 strobes, Kodachrome 64 film.

ingredient you need for good pictures. Find out from your travel agent or tour operator the optimum time of year to dive in your selected area. Basically, you'll want to go in the dry season and when the water is calm and clear. This varies from site to site. Keep in mind that predicting the weather is not an exact science. For example, my wife and I visited Palau in mid-January in the middle of the dry season in 1991, and it rained all day, every day, for a week! So, in addition to planning, you'll need some luck—and you'll need to be patient when nature does not cooperate.

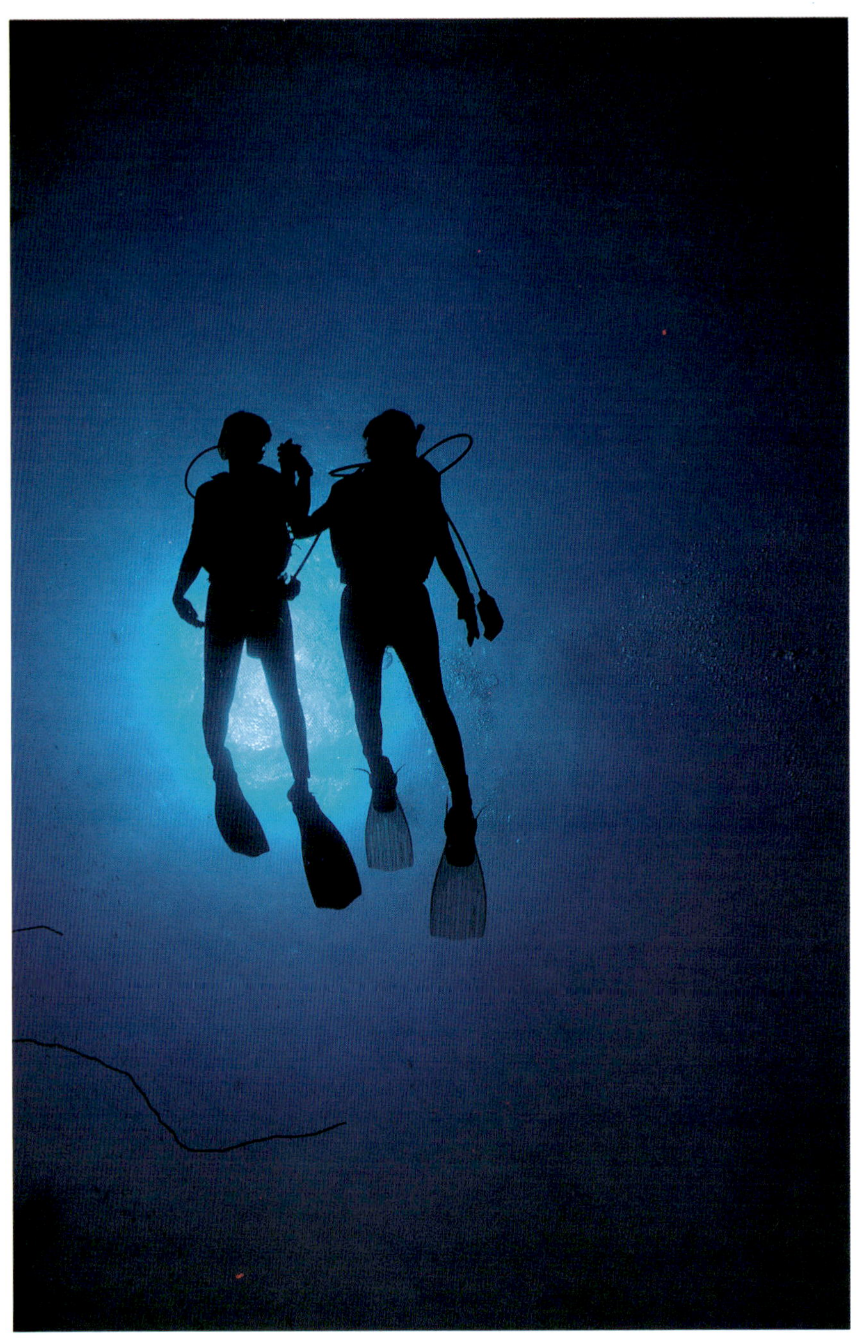

Bring a buddy along to share your underwater experiences.

Chapter 5: What to Bring on Your Dive Trip— Essential Accessories

Your camera body, lenses, and strobe aren't all you'll need. Use this checklist to complete your preparing and packing.

In addition to all your scuba and camera gear, there are certain items that fall into the "don't leave home without it" category. These things are on my dive trip packing checklist, and I recommend that you put them on yours.

Repair items: I never go on a trip without these three items: duct tape, super glue, and rubber bands. I have used duct tape for holding broken strobe arms in place and for attaching filters to strobes. Super glue has held broken diving masks and camera housing parts in place (but don't use it for water-tight seals). And rubber bands are great for tying down loose strobe sync cords. I'm sure you can think of one hundred more uses for these items— especially when you're on a dive trip, miles away from the nearest hardware store.

Seasickness pills: Did you know there are two stages to being seasick? First stage: You feel like you are going to die. Second stage: You wish you were dead. Believe me, this expression is true. I've been there. To help avoid feeding the fish my breakfast, I use an over-the-counter pill called Bonine. This nondrowsy, chewable pill keeps me feeling good even in pretty rough seas. Other nondrowsy formulas are available both over the counter and from doctors. It is important not to take anything that causes drowsiness, which ultimately affects your performance under water. Such medications are not recommended for scuba divers.

Sunscreen: Unless you want to look like a lobster and feel like a French fry,

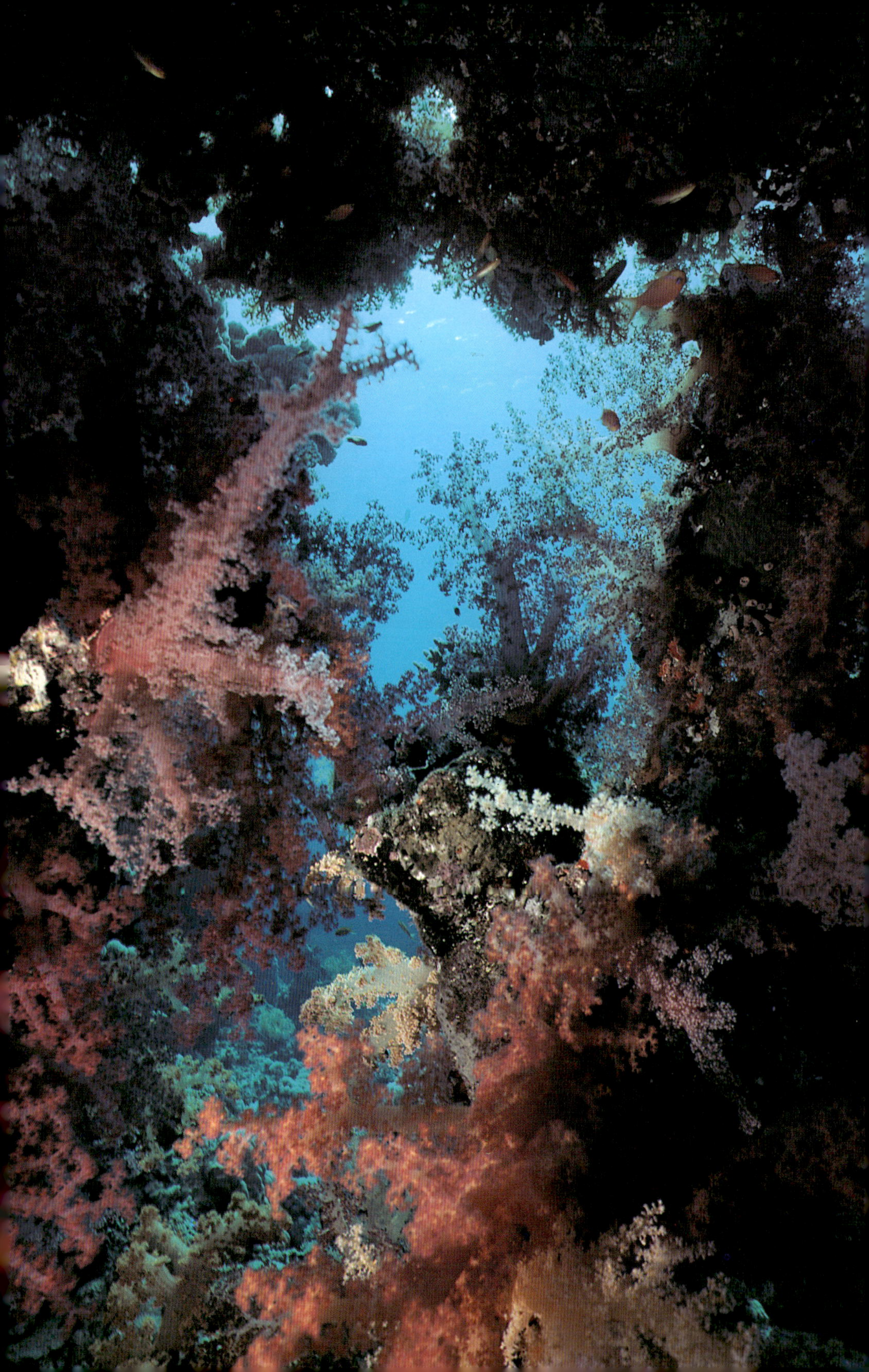

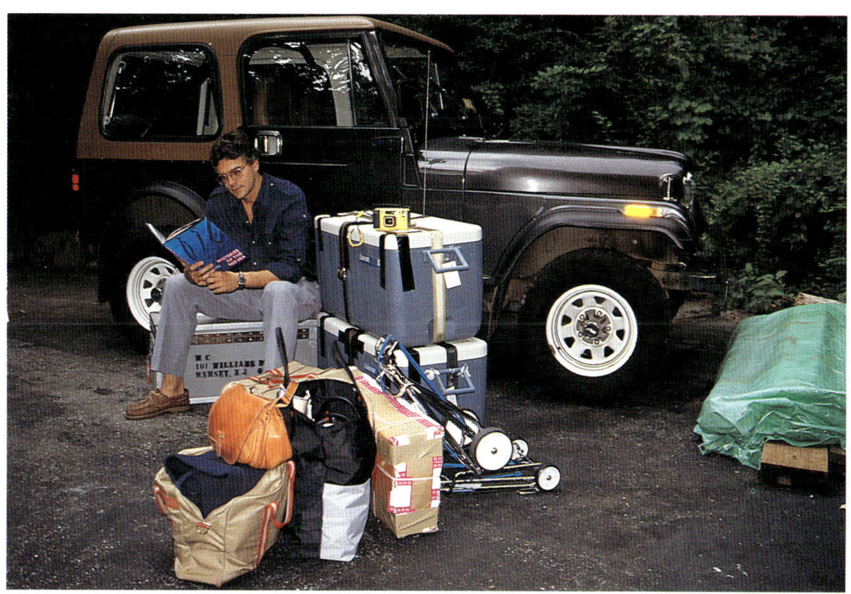

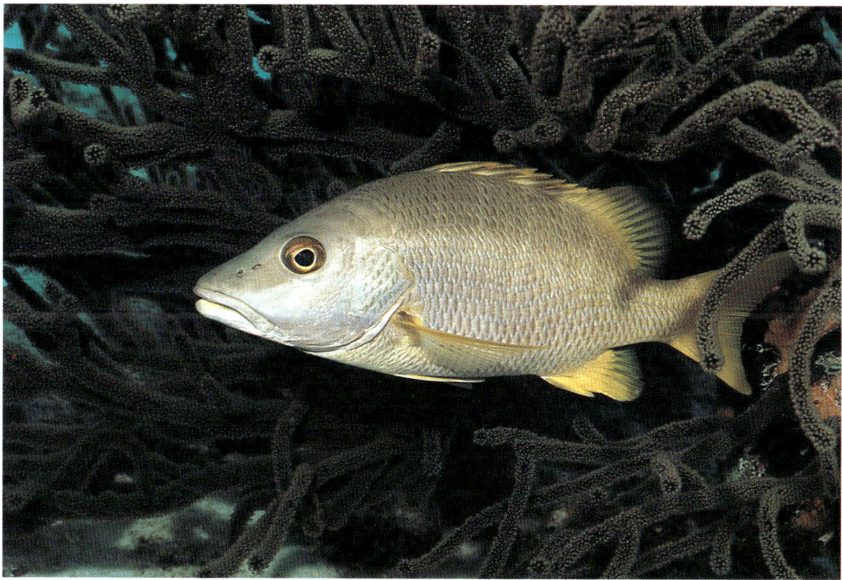

TOP: When my wife Susan and I go on assignment, we bring enough photo equipment, scuba gear, clothes, and medical supplies for a mini army. The point is this: Be prepared for the unexpected! ABOVE: **Subject:** Grunt. **Site:** Bonaire, Netherlands Antilles. **Equipment and film:** Nikonos RS, 50mm lens, Nikonos SB-103 strobe, Kodak Elite 100. OPPOSITE: **Subject:** Soft corals. **Site:** Red Sea, Ras Mohammed. **Equipment and film:** Nikonos V, 15mm lens, two Nikonos SB-103 strobes, Kodachrome 64.

use a waterproof sunblock (at least SPF 15). Apply this before you leave your resort room or boat cabin, and you'll not only feel better on your trip, you'll also look better when you're in your 60s. Also, don't forget your hat and shades. These are two important accessories when on the water, where glare can make the sun's ultraviolet rays twice as dangerous.

Money: No joke. Most divers bring too many clothes and not enough money. At dive resorts and on live-aboard boats, all you need is a few T-shirts and pairs of shorts. On the other hand, you'll probably want to buy lots of new T-shirts and local handicrafts for you and your family—so bring extra cash or travelers' checks.

Batteries and film: When it comes to batteries and film, I suggest packing more than you think you'll need. First of all, most underwater photographers (me, too) over shoot simply because of the beauty they find beneath the waves. This burns up batteries as well as film. If these essential accessories are available at your dive site, you'll probably pay much more than you would have paid at home. And, if you are in Pago Pago or some other remote location, film and batteries may not be available. Also, remember that if you plan to use a nicad unit for your strobe and are destined for other countries, pack a voltage converter.

My basic rule of thumb for calculating the number of rolls I need is this: For each dive I can possibly make (sometimes five a day), I pack one roll of film for each camera. Then, I pack another five rolls just in case I drop a roll overboard or tear the sprockets while loading. So, if I plan to make five dives for five days—for a total of twenty-five dives—with two cameras, I take fifty-five rolls of thirty-six-exposure film. (Don't take twenty-four-exposure film; you'll run out of exposures before you're through your dive.)

Knife and light: I never go on a trip without my Swiss Army knife and a small top-side flashlight. The knife has saved the day on more than one occasion when I had to open something (I fondly remember a cool Belekin beer in Belize), and the light has guided me to the "head" (diver talk for the bathroom) in remote island reserves when the generator was turned off for the evening.

54

Personal care kit: Only once did I not hand-carry my toiletries with me on the plane. This was the time my luggage was lost on my way to Siberia. So, for fourteen days, I did not have my electric shaver, and I cut the hell out of my face with a Siberian straight edge. In addition, I did not have my vitamins or any other of my personal care products. Because deodorant is nonexistent in Siberia and soap is scarce, I did not smell like a rose before and after my diving adventures. Lesson learned: Always hand-carry important stuff, including a first-aid kit.

Antidiarrheal medicine: Want a 100-percent foolproof way to avoid the "runs" in exotic locations? Stay home. Yes, it's true. Sooner or later, you'll get that sinking feeling that something is not right. Again, I've been there—most recently in a small plane with no bathroom. An over-the-counter product called Imodium-AD takes away the symptoms almost immediately. Pack it. Period.

Dry box: Dive stores sell waterproof dry boxes in a variety of sizes. These O-ring–sealed, plastic boxes are great for keeping small items—sunglasses, wallet, extra O-rings, O-ring grease, lens cleaning tissue, diver certification card, snacks, etc.—dry while traveling around on boats. If your dry box does fall in the water, it will float. If it's yellow, it will be easy to find.

Glow sticks: When diving at night, I always tie a Cyalume (chemical glow stick) on my tank. This way, even if my dive light goes out on a pitch-dark night, the boat crew can spot me when I surface. I pack one Cyalume for each night dive I can possibly make. You can buy these life-savers at most dive shops.

Bug spray: The beautiful ads and colorful editorials in the dive magazines don't talk about this, but around tropical reefs, the next most prolific creatures to fish are bugs—mosquitoes, sand fleas (also called no see 'ems), and the like. If you use bug spray, you'll sleep better at night.

Passport: If you travel to a foreign country, it is quite possible that you can lose your passport or have it stolen from you. When I travel, I always keep a photocopy of the front page of my passport, which has all of the pertinent information needed for replacement, in a suitcase or a camera bag. This way, if my passport is lost, it will be much easier to get a new one—and get home. Additional passport photos of yourself are also a very good idea whenever traveling abroad.

Patience: If you don't know what the terms "Mexican time" or "Caribbean time" mean, you may find out on your dive trip. Often, things run on schedule, but there are times when you have to muster all your patience when boat (and plane) departures are postponed. If you leave home with a patient attitude, you'll avoid frustration when you encounter unexpected changes in schedules.

As you'll see in the next chapter, when shooting with a strobe, you should bracket your shots to ensure recording the true color of a subject. The photo on the opposite page shows the true color of the orange sponge, while the photo at right, which is slightly underexposed, shows it as red-orange. **Subject:** Foreground, orange sponge. Background, purple tube sponge. **Site:** Bonaire, Netherlands Antilles. **Equipment and film:** Nikonos RS, 20–35mm zoom lens set at 20mm, Nikonos SB-104 strobe, Kodak Elite 100.

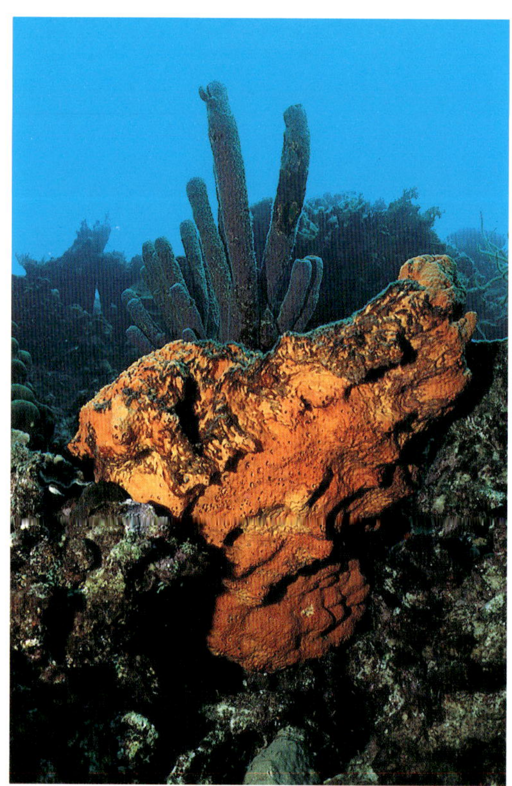

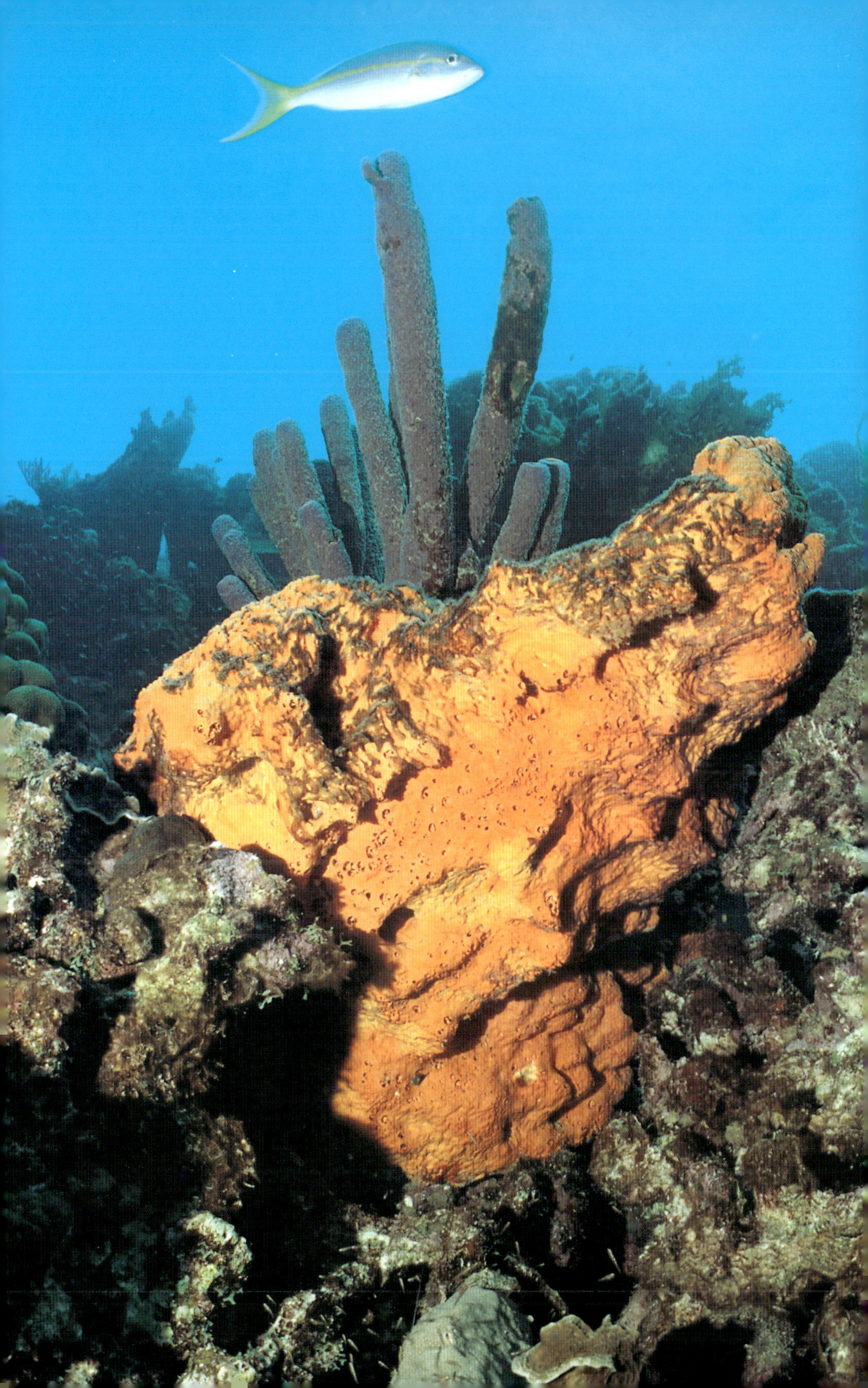

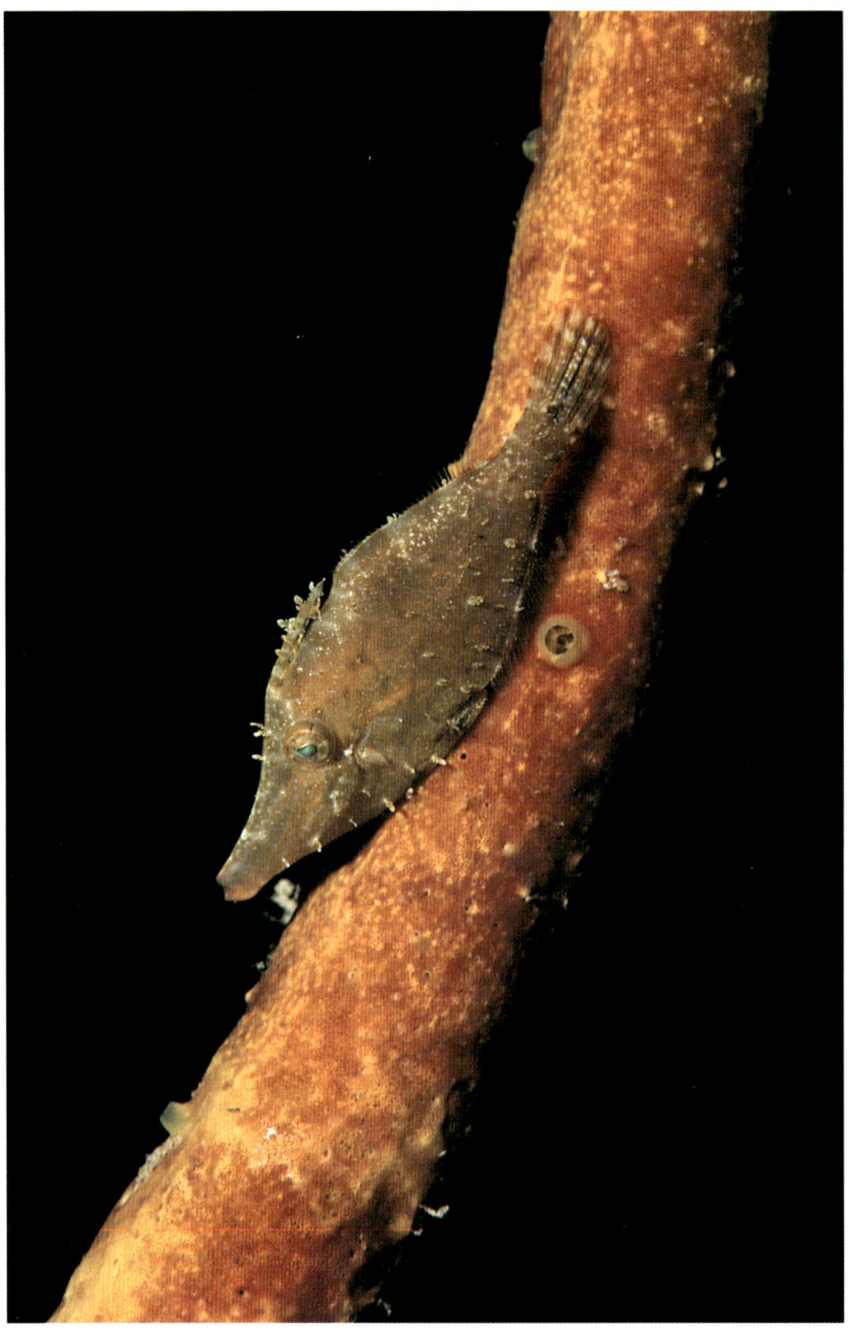

When you want your subjects to stand out, plain backgrounds are most effective.
Subject: Sleeping sharpnose pufferfish. **Site:** Bonaire, Netherlands Antilles.
Equipment and film: Nikonos RS, 50mm lens, Nikonos SB-104 strobe, Kodak Elite
100.

Chapter 6: The Basics

What every underwater photographer needs to know—common sense, composition, and creativity.

In underwater photography, as in all photography, knowing the basics is the key to good pictures. It doesn't matter whether you have a one-camera Nikonos system or an ultra-sophisticated 35mm autofocus SLR in an underwater housing, the following list of "basics" will help you get great shots rather than snapshots.

Know how to dive: Before a diver goes into the water with a camera, he or she should be comfortable in the water with dive gear and diving in general. Going into the water with a lot of camera gear may be frustrating and, unless you're accustomed to extra pieces of equipment, potentially dangerous.

You can get a "C" (certification) card from any of several organizations, including PADI (Professional Association of Diving Instructors), NAUI (National Association of Underwater Instructors), and through your local YMCA. These groups offer ten-week courses that will teach you all the basics of diving. (If you plan to try underwater photography, I definitely *do not* recommend on-site mini classes offered by resorts that teach you to dive in a day or two. Realistically, your skills as a diver after only a day or two won't enable you to handle all that photographic gear.)

After you learn how to dive and have purchased a camera system, I recommend a pool session with all your camera and scuba gear. In calm pool conditions, you'll be able to get a feeling of what it is like to dive will all your equipment. Remember, however, that diving in open water, with currents and surge, is more arduous than pool diving.

Research: By reading about your diving destination and studying underwater pictures of the area before your dive trip, you'll get a good idea of the kind of marine life you'll encounter, so you can choose which lenses you'll need, such as macro for small subjects, wide-angle for schooling fish, etc.

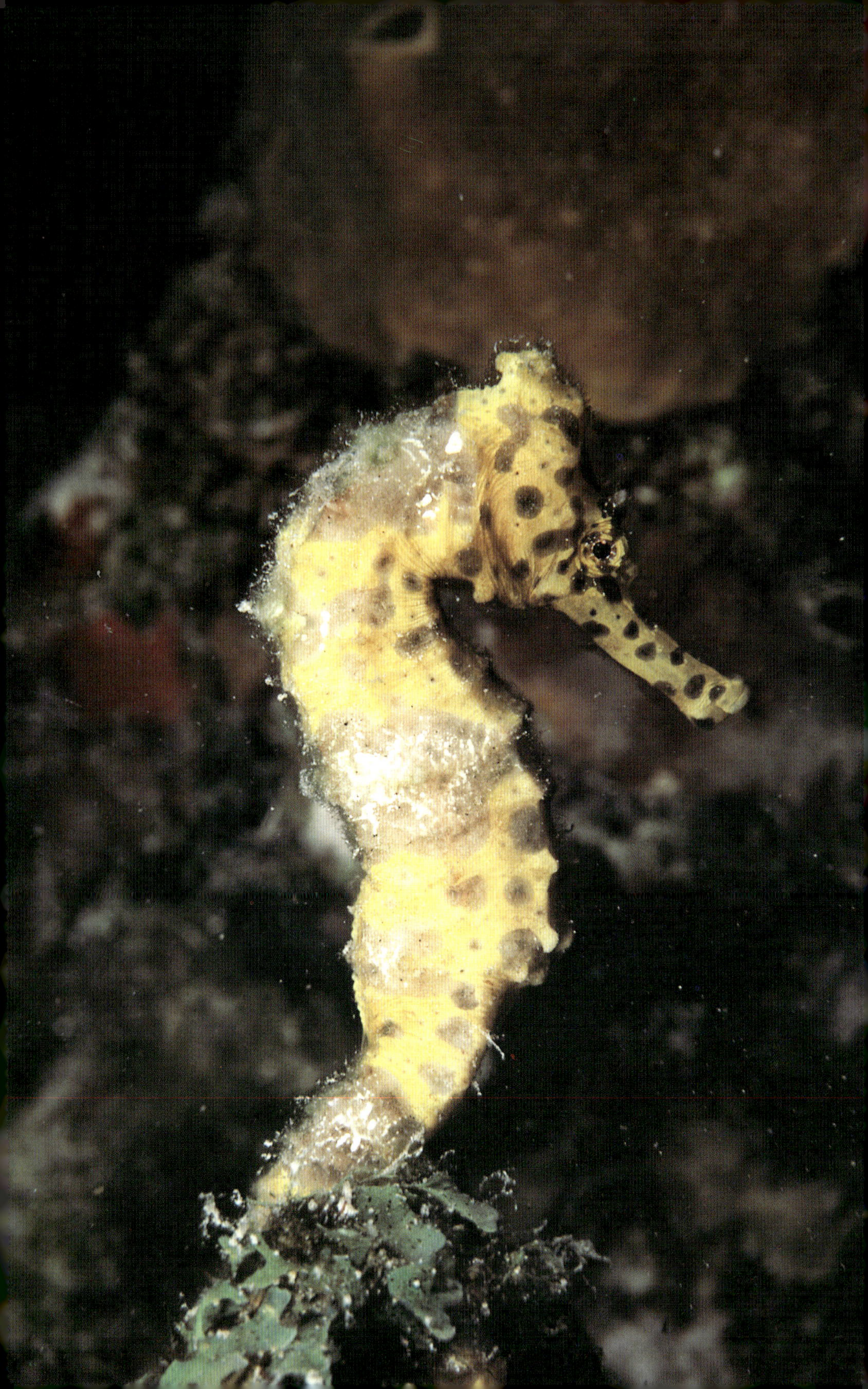

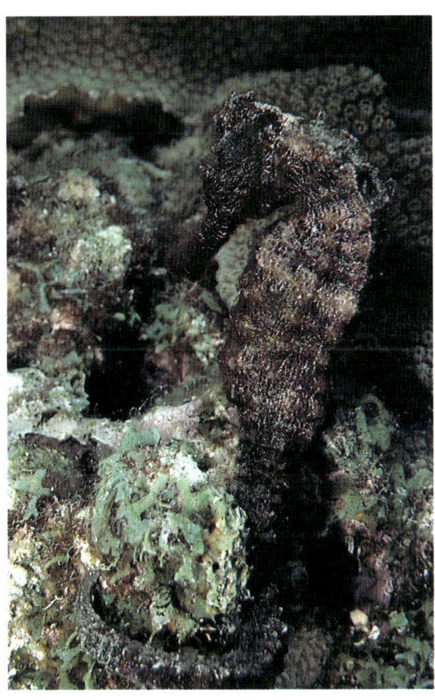

ABOVE AND OPPOSITE: Shy subjects are best photographed with your camera set on automatic—if you fill most of the frame with your subject. This technique will help your camera's through-the-lens flash metering system get a correct exposure. **(For both photos): Subject:** Sea horses. **Site:** Bonaire, Netherlands Antilles. **Equipment and film:** Nikonos RS, 50mm lens, Nikonos SB-104 strobe, Kodak Elite 100.

Don't dive deep: You'll get the brightest natural light pictures with the most color if you stay shallow. That's because color decreases as depth increases. If you stay shallow, you can get some great natural light pictures, as well as pictures in which you can mix daylight with artificial strobe light.

Understand shutter speeds and *f*-stops: These two camera controls give you creative exposure control of your pictures.

The shutter speed indicates the length of time the shutter remains open. The faster the shutter speed, the greater chance you'll have of "freezing" your subject's motion in natural light photography. In most natural light situations, a shutter speed of 1/250 second is fast enough to freeze the action of swimming fish. To ensure a sharp picture, shoot at the highest shutter speed possible.

The *f*-stop controls the amount of light passing through the lens and determines how much of the scene is in focus. Smaller *f*-stops (larger numbers) provide greater depth of field than larger *f*-stops (smaller numbers). For maximum depth of field, shoot at the smallest *f*-stop possible.

Composition: Autofocus and auto-exposure cameras offer underwater photographers many benefits, including the ability to concentrate on composition rather than having to spend time adjusting knobs and dials before pressing the shutter release button.

One of the key ingredients to good composition, in both wide-angle and close-up underwater photography (and all photography for that matter), is the background. When photographing a swimming fish, try to photograph the fish in open water or against a relatively plain background. If a fish is photographed against a busy background of vertical and/or horizontal coral branches, not only will the photograph lose impact, but the background will be very distracting to the viewer. Granted, composing an underwater picture with a relatively plain background is not always possible, so it's important to remember that a photograph that is less than perfect (in your opinion) is better than no photo at all.

It's also important to remember that there is a time when a busy background can enhance a fish portrait, such as when you want to illustrate the camouflage coloring of a certain species. In this situation, both the background and subject should be in sharp focus.

Another composition element to be aware of is the brightness level of the objects in the background. If they are brighter than the main subject, they will be distracting. One ex-

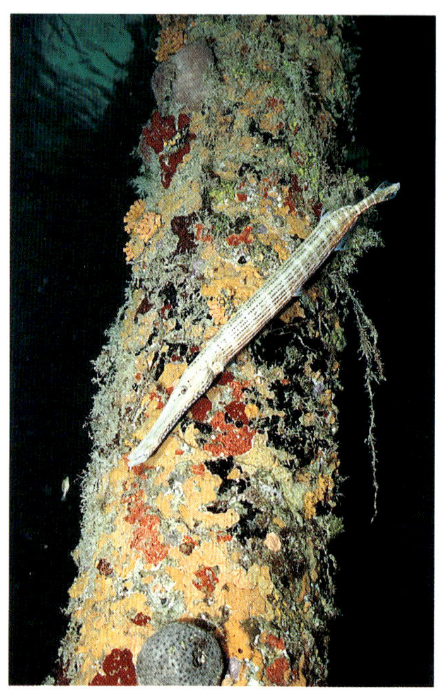

ABOVE AND OPPOSITE: When shooting slide film, bracketing is essential if you want the perfect exposure. To bracket, take pictures over and under the recommended setting. The photo above is overexposed by one stop, but the photo opposite is right on. **Subject:** Trumpetfish. **Site:** Bonaire Town Pier, Netherlands Antilles. **Equipment and film:** Nikonos RS, 20–35mm zoom lens set at 20mm, Nikonos SB-104 strobe, Kodak Elite 100.

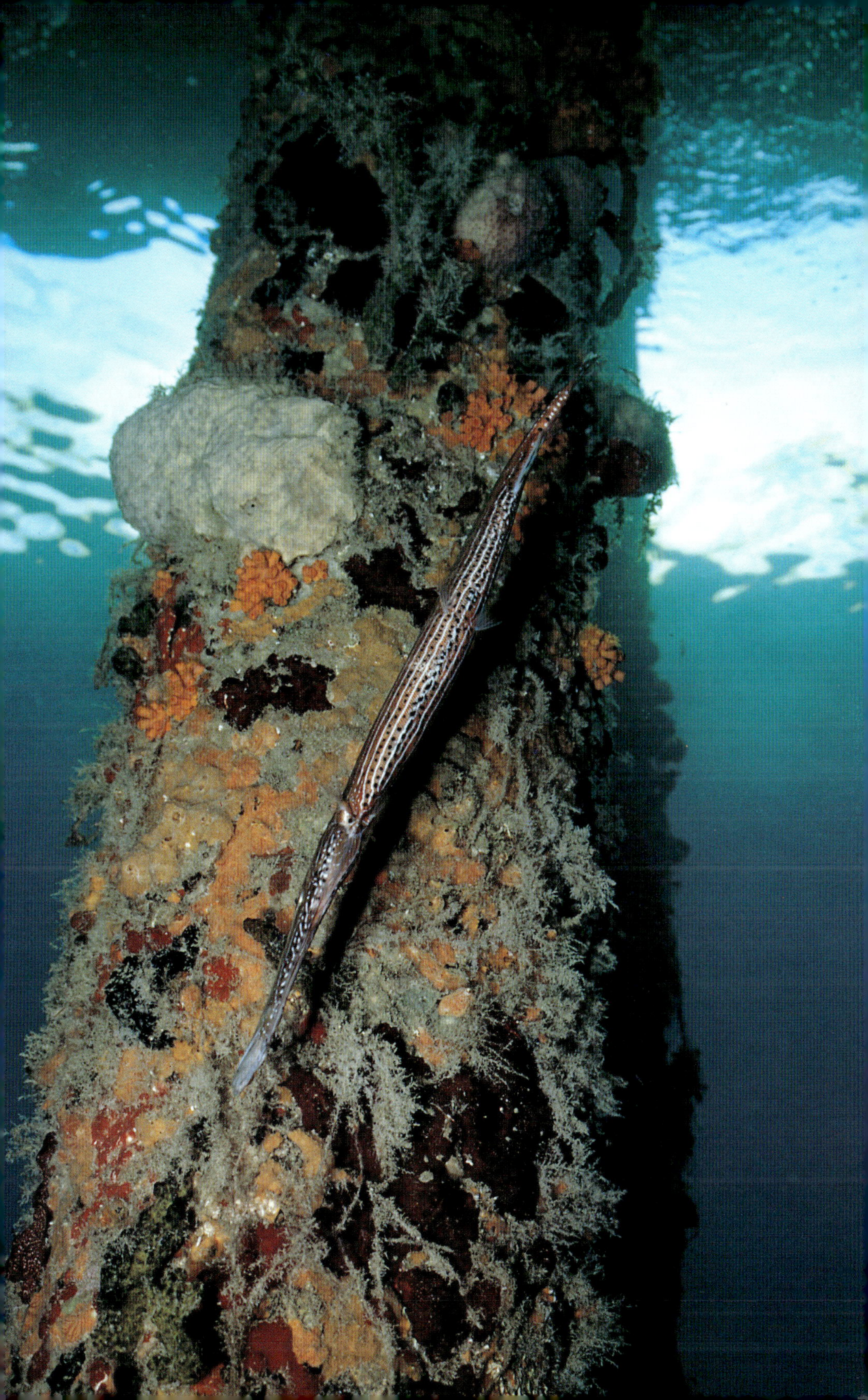

ception is a photograph of a diver or fish swimming in front of a bright underwater sunburst. To help you remember the importance of the brightness of background elements, think of this: When someone views a picture, the eye goes to the brightest element in the photograph first.

Another important thing to remember about composition is that the subject does not always have to be in the center of the frame. One school of thought suggests that you view the scene in your viewfinder as though the lines of a tick-tack-toe board are placed over the scene, and that you compose your picture with the main subject placed at one of the points where the lines intersect. Another technique is to have a fish or diver positioned off center, so that it looks as if the subject is swimming into the scene.

If you have time, try composing a picture in several different ways. Then shoot the one or ones you like the best.

(For more discussion on composition, see "Capturing the Wide View—Naturally and with a Strobe," and "Shooting Close-ups—Day and Night.")

Shoot on automatic for starters: Camera manufacturers spend big bucks on developing automatic exposure programs that will deliver good results in a variety of situations. Novice underwater photographers will get a much higher percentage of good pictures when they shoot on automatic than they will making time-consuming, manual adjustments.

Bracket your exposures: By making exposures one stop over and one stop under the setting suggested in the automatic or manual mode, you're bound to get a good exposure.

The easiest way to bracket is by adjusting the ISO dial. For example, when using ISO 100 speed film, setting the ISO dial at 200 will technically give you a one-stop underexposed image, and setting the ISO dial at 50 will technically give you a one-stop overexposed image. Out of the three frames, one will most likely be the one you like. However, remember to set the ISO dial back to the original position after each sequence.

When shooting with your camera set on manual, use the recommended setting by adjusting the *f*-stop and shutter speed accordingly. Now, you can bracket by adjusting either the *f*-stop or shutter speed. To bracket with the *f*-stop, take additional exposures one stop over and one stop under the recommended setting. To further fine tune your exposures, you can bracket in half stops. To bracket with the shutter speed, take additional exposures at the next higher and then the next lower shutter speed.

Look for color: Color makes underwater pictures come alive. Try composing wide-angle scenes with a yellow sea lily, purple sea fan, or red sea whip in the corner or bottom of the frame. Not only will this enhance the scene, but the foreground element will add a sense of depth to your picture. Along the same line of thought, try to avoid including dull subjects, such as dead coral or algae-covered coral heads, in any portion of the frame.

Don't despair: Many first-time underwater shooters are disappointed with their results, thinking that they should have gotten thirty-six perfectly exposed, expertly composed images—all with bright colors and sharp detail. However, since many professional underwater photographers (and I include myself in this group) are happy with one great shot per roll, don't get too discouraged if it takes more than a few dives to perfect your underwater shooting techniques.

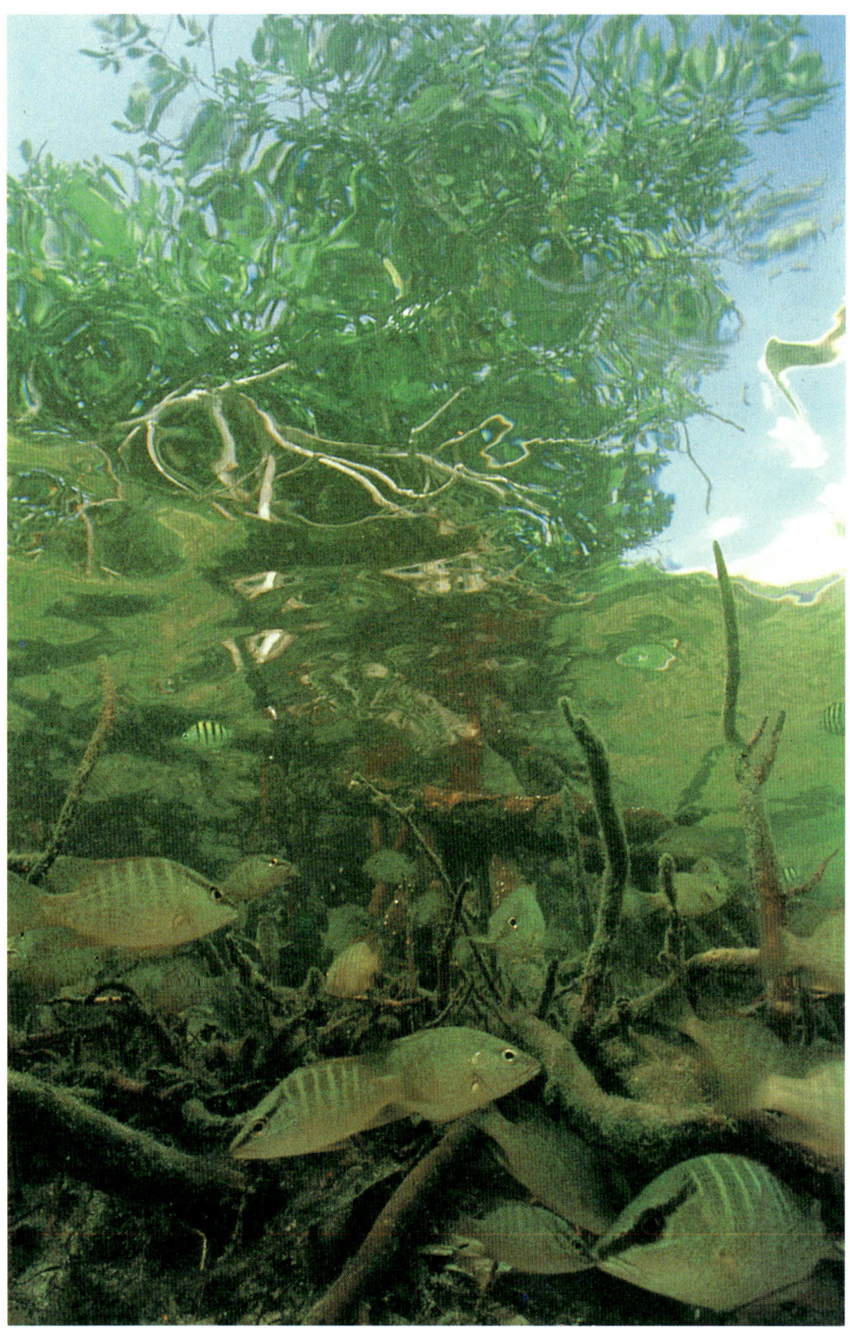

Underwater photo opportunities begin just inches below the water's surface. **Subject:** Mangroves and snappers. **Site:** Belize, Central America. **Equipment and film:** Nikonos V, 15mm lens, Ektachrome 400.

Chapter 7: The Under-water Environment— A Photographer's View

How the marine environment—water clarity, weather, angle of the sun, subject size, and subject color— affects picture taking.

Before you begin taking underwater pictures, you need to know how the marine environment—which is approximately eight hundred times more dense than air and is filled with millions of ever-present floating plants and animals—affects picture taking and picture-taking opportunities. Basically, the things you need to consider are: water clarity, weather, angle of the sun, subject size, and subject color.

Visibility and weather conditions: If you want to get clear wide-angle pictures, you must have good underwater visibility, usually considered to be one hundred or more feet. In most cases, you'll need to dive in the tropics (about 30 degrees north and south of the equator) to get clear water. In most northern and southern locations, there are so many nutrients and so much plankton in the water that visibility is usually limited to only a few feet. Antarctica is one saltwater exception and Lake Baikal in Siberia is a freshwater exception. In these two locations, visibility can exceed two hundred feet.

Weather conditions also affect how much you'll see and be able to photograph underwater. If it's windy and the water is choppy, much of the light is lost by scattered reflection from the surface. Because less light penetrates the water, visibility and maximum shooting distance, as well as subject contrast, are decreased. Wind also stirs up particles in the water, reducing visibility.

Overcast and cloudy skies also affect visibility. For example, on a sunny day in the tropics, visibility may be one hundred feet at noon. A completely

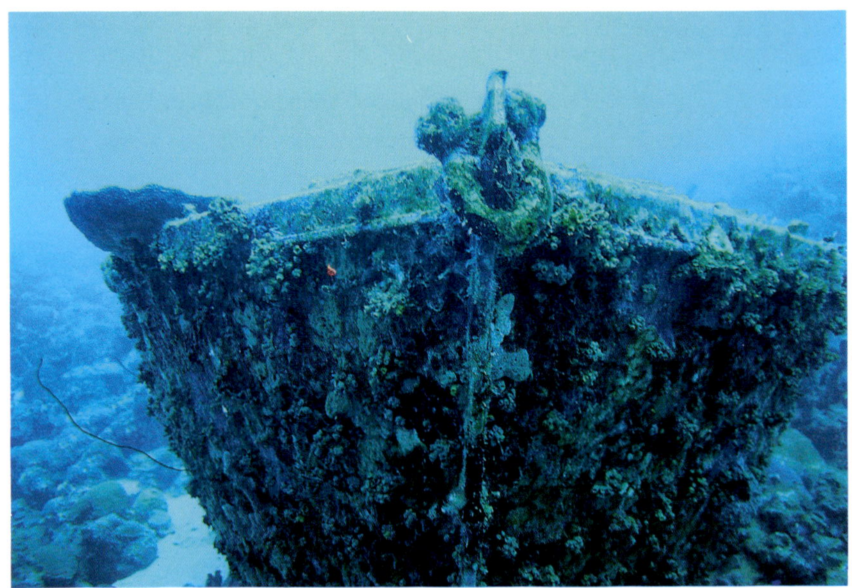

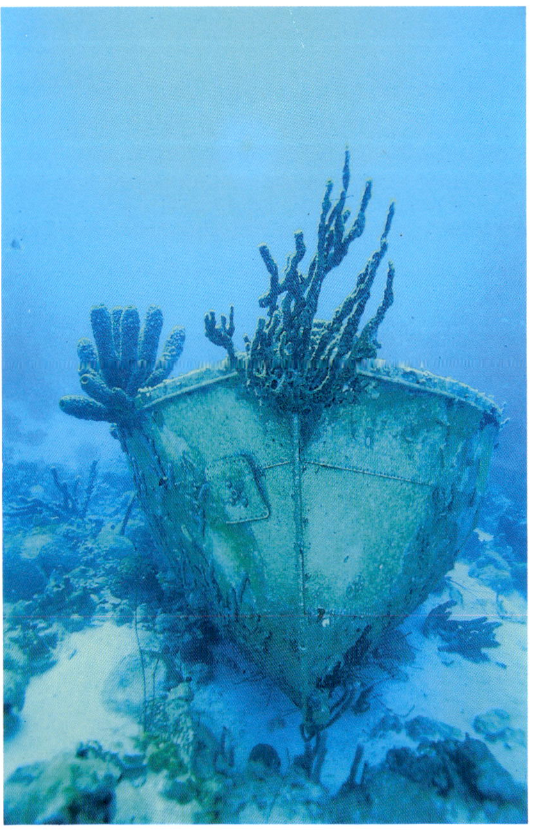

ABOVE, LEFT, AND OPPOSITE: Under water, color drops off rapidly, starting with the reds at ten feet. At seventy feet, as illustrated in this series, even colorful subjects take on a blue tint. The photos above and left were taken in natural light, and those opposite were taken with two strobe units. **Subject:** Sunken rowboat. **Site:** Bonaire, Netherlands Antilles. **Equipment and film:** Nikon 8008s, Stromm One underwater housing, 20mm lens, two Nikonos SB-103 strobes, Kodak Elite 100.

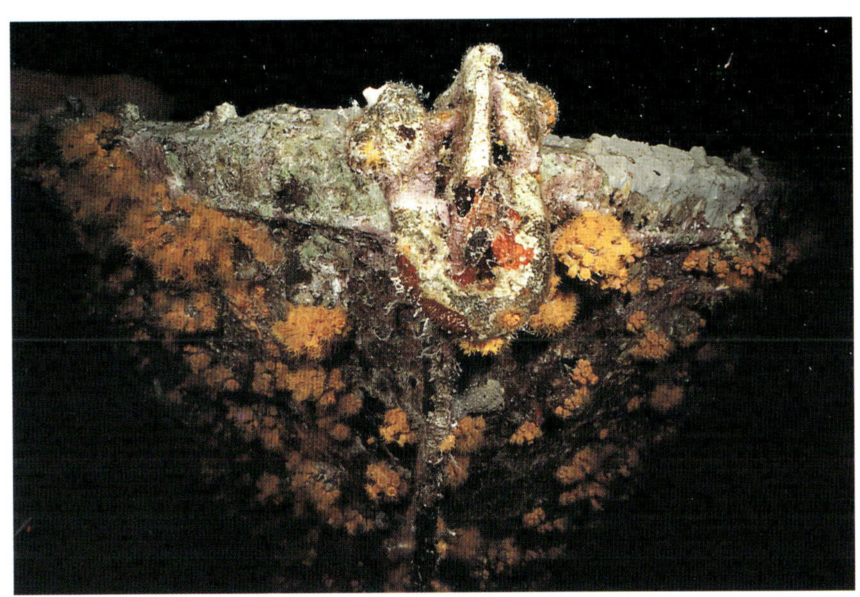

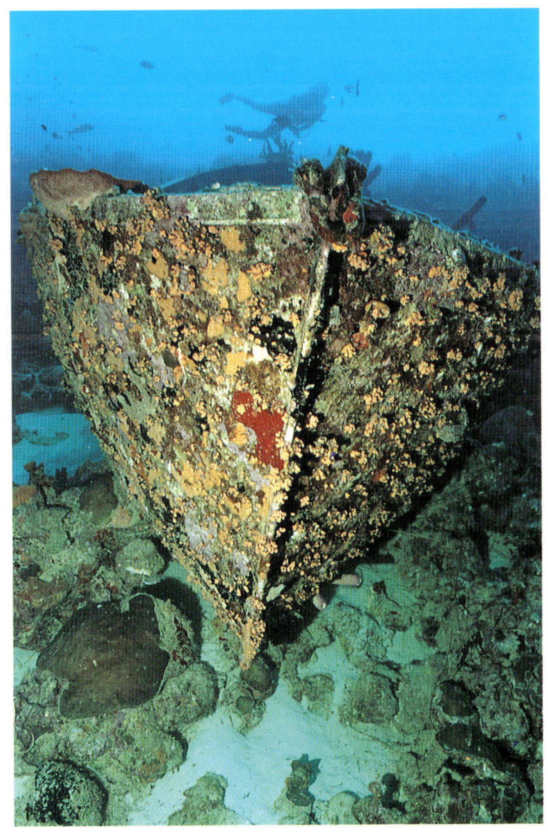

overcast sky can reduce this to thirty or forty feet.

Before you make arrangements for a dive, check the weather conditions or "reef report." If the report is bad, it may be better to relax around the hotel or local town until the wind dies down and the sun comes out.

Best time to dive: The best time to dive for wide-angle, natural light pictures is between 10:00 AM and 2:00 PM. During these hours, sunlight has to penetrate the least amount of water because the sun is relatively high in the sky. Therefore, it's brighter down below. In the early morning and late-afternoon hours, when the sun is very low, more sunlight is reflected off the surface, with less light illuminating the underwater world. This reduces visibility.

Noon is the ideal time to dive for natural light, wide-angle pictures. If possible, try to schedule your dive so that you are in the water at this time. When taking close-up photographs, the time of day does not matter because you'll be shooting very close to your subjects, with a strobe.

Subject size: Light rays behave differently in media of different densities. In water, objects appear nearer and larger than they would at the same distance in air. If you have ever stood in a swimming pool and looked down at your strangely short-looking legs, you have experienced this effect. Your feet suddenly look larger and closer, due to the refraction of light.

The apparent change in subject size caused by refraction can lead to focusing errors (if you are not using an autofocus camera). Refraction causes objects to look about 25 percent closer under water than they actually are. For example, if a subject is actually about eight feet away from you, it will appear to be about six feet away. Thus, it is important to take extra time when setting the distance scale on nonautofocus lenses.

Color loss: One of the biggest disappointments to the beginning underwater photographer is the absence of color in his or her natural light photographs. You see and photograph purple sea fans, green sponges, pink sweepers, orange cup corals, and yellow tail snappers. However, when the pictures come back from the lab, you wonder where all the color has gone and why your pictures have a blue tint.

The answer to this perplexing question is simple: Water filters out colors selectively. The deeper you dive, the more colors you lose. The red component of the light starts to go first. In clear water, it is completely filtered out at approximately fifteen feet. Orange is completely filtered out at about eighteen feet. Yellow goes at forty-five feet.

As a general rule, if you plan to shoot natural light pictures deeper than ten feet, use a CC 30R or Underwater Pro color correction filter, which will "restore" some, but not all, of the lost color. Another option would be to use Ektachrome Underwater film. (See also the chapter "Choosing the Right Film.")

False color: Why does a diver still see reds, yellows, purples, and a wealth of other colors at depths where we know they are filtered out? It's because the eyes and brain play tricks on the mind under water.

For example, if you are diving with a buddy who you know is wearing a red wet suit, you'll see the red suit, perhaps even at forty feet. Your brain knows it's red, so you see it as red. The film, however, does not know it's red and records it as blue.

Here's another example of false color. When you are diving and recognize a yellow tail snapper from a close-up photo you've seen in a book, you will see the fish as yellow, even at a depth of fifty feet. In reality, the color is filtered out, so you don't see the yellow. However, if you have no previous knowledge of the yellow tail, it will appear bluish.

The above example is, of course, an oversimplification of the very complex topic of vision. However, it makes a pertinent point: The way to accurately record colors under water is to use a strobe close to your subject. Remember, the closer the light source is to the subject, the fewer colors are filtered out by the water. (See also "Selecting the Right Strobe.")

By taking the aforementioned conditions and variables into consideration, you'll be able to maximize the productivity of your picture-taking time under water.

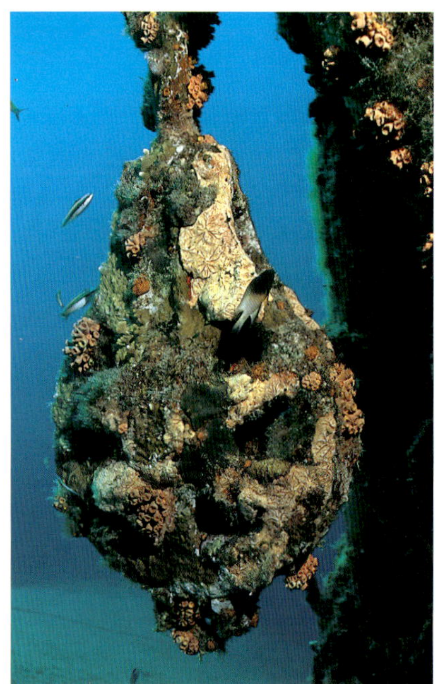

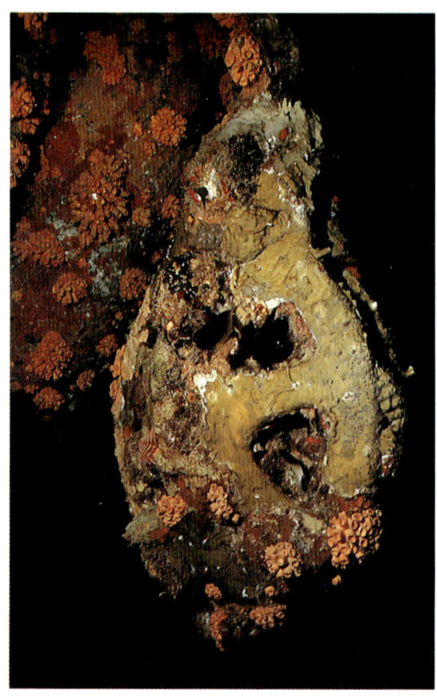

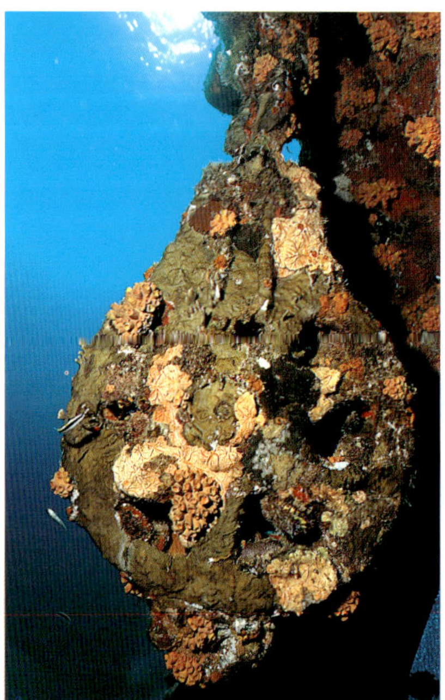

ABOVE AND LEFT: Do these look like midday, midnight, and early morning pictures to you? Actually, they were taken at midday within seconds of each other. The difference is that I selected a different shutter speed for each exposure. I shot the top left photo at 1/30 second, the above photo at 1/125 second, and the bottom left photo at 1/15 second. By angling the camera toward the surface for this last shot, I created the impression of an early morning dive. **Subject:** Deadeye. **Site:** *Helma Hooker* wreck, Bonaire, Netherlands Antilles. **Equipment and film:** Nikonos RS, 20–35mm zoom lens set at 20mm, Nikonos SB-104 strobe, Kodachrome 64.

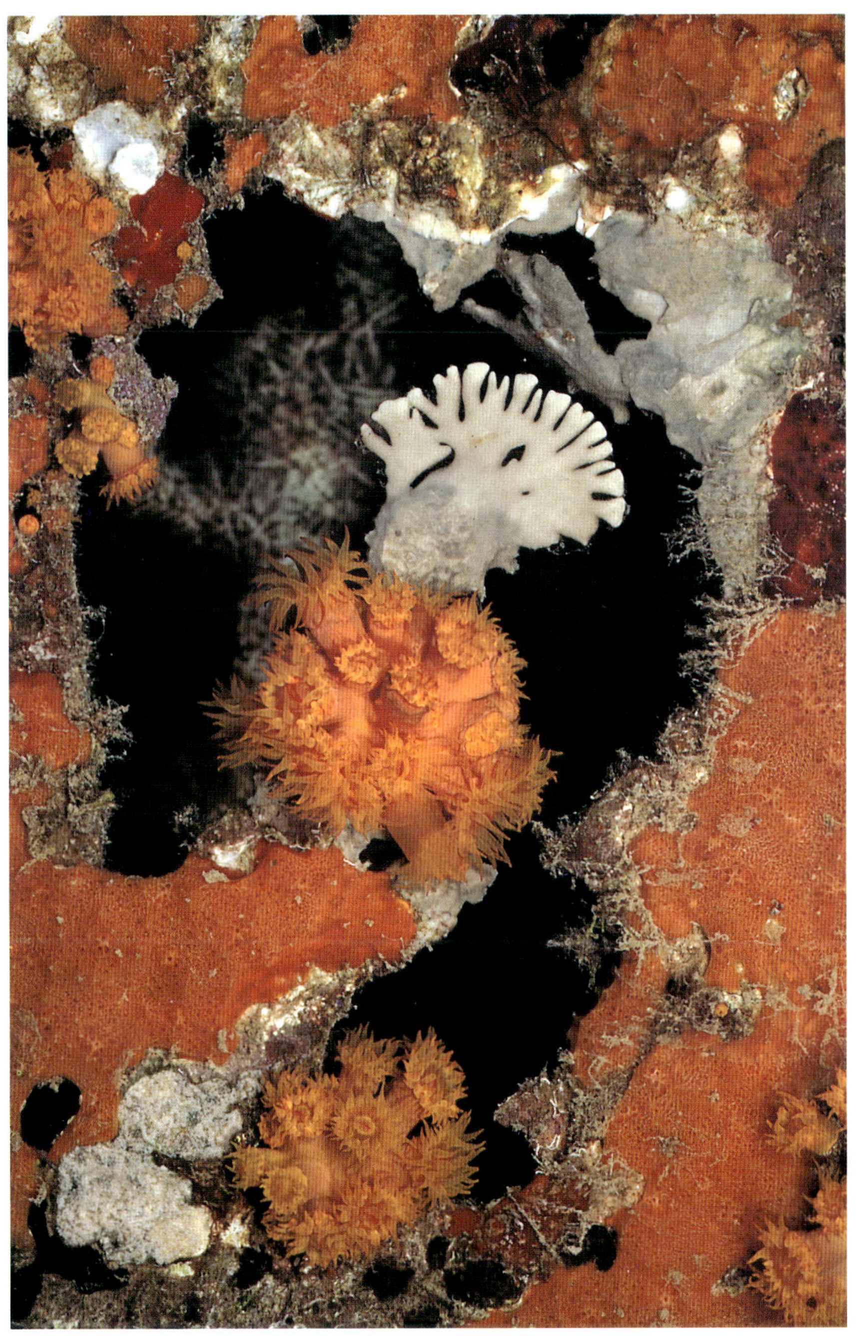

Under water, you'll find an endless number of patterns in nature to photograph. **Subject:** Rusted hull of a shipwreck. **Site:** Bonaire, Netherlands Antilles. **Equipment and film:** Nikonos RS, 50mm lens, Nikonos SB-104 strobe, Kodak Elite 100.

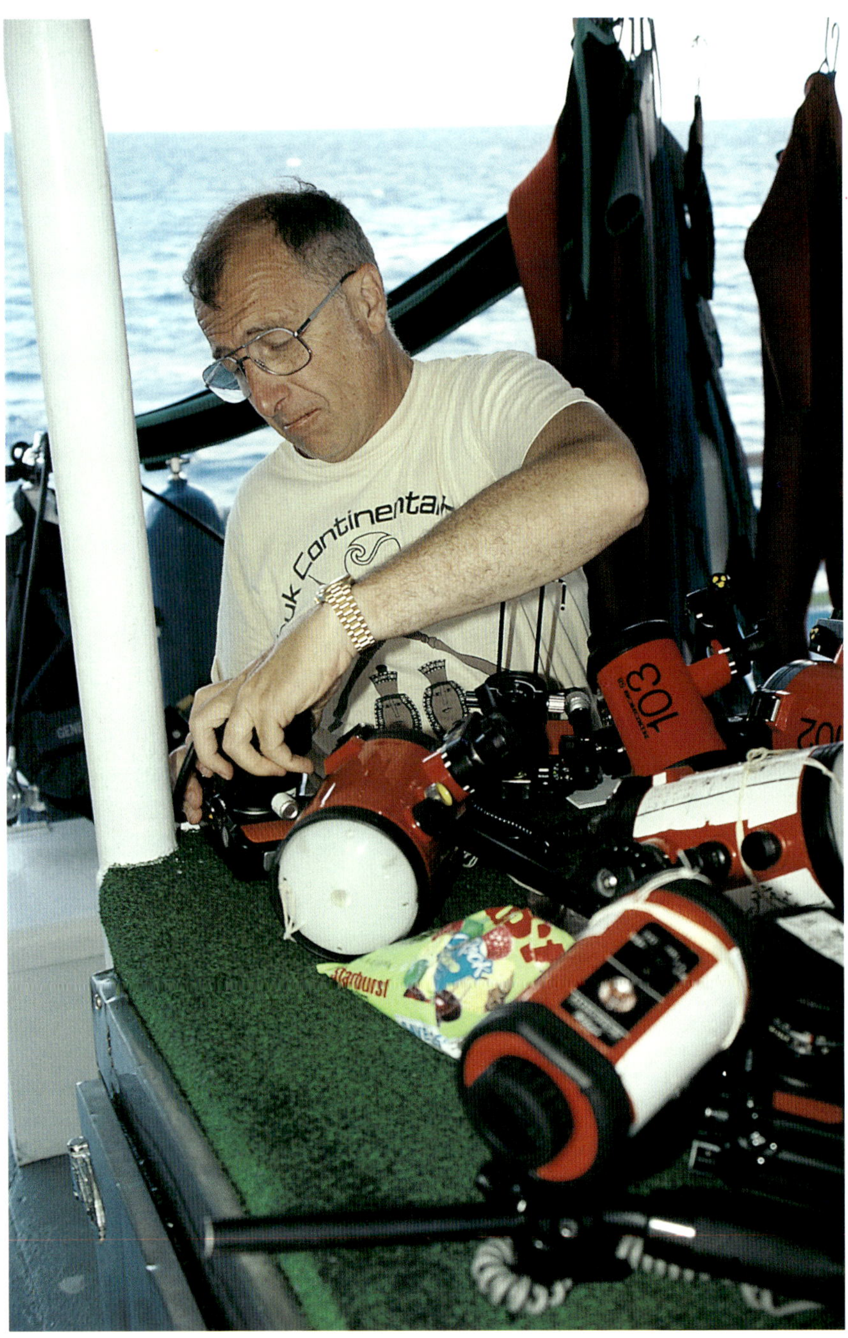

Camera tables on live-aboard boats are the best places to clean your camera—before and after your dive. Just be sure to mark your camera so it doesn't get lost in the crowd.

Chapter 8: Camera Care—Before and After Your Dive

The right stuff for your camera and equipment so that you'll enjoy years of good pictures.

Underwater cameras and housings are designed to be foolproof and flood proof. However, to deliver years of good pictures, cameras still need proper maintenance and some TLC (tender loving care). Photographers need an understanding of what cameras can and cannot do. In this section, you'll find some pretty basic stuff—stuff that can save the day on your dive trip.

Don't over-grease your O-rings: This may sound like a minor recommendation, but it's essential to keeping your camera and film dry. O-rings are the round rubber gaskets that keep water from entering the joints in an underwater camera, housing, or strobe. O-ring grease actually attracts dirt, sand, and grime. Therefore, if you use a lot of grease, you'll increase the chance of getting tiny particles on the O-ring that can break the seal and cause a big flood inside your camera. Also, it's highly advisable to re-grease the camera back O-ring after each roll of film. (See your instruction manual for details.)

Check and double-check your lenses and sync cords: Lenses and sync cords have a tendency to become loose or twisted. This is especially true with the relatively heavy Nikonos 15mm lens. Before your dive, make sure all your sync cords are tightened. Also, check your Nikonos lens to see that it is seated properly in the camera body. If it's not, it can twist off under water—which happened to me. Once.

Rewind the film as soon as possible: Probably every underwater photographer has opened the camera back without rewinding the film, ruining irreplaceable, precious photos. At the end of the roll, rewind the film back into the canister, even if you don't plan to load a new roll right away.

Keep your camera out of the sun: The strong rays of the sun can damage your camera, dry out the O-rings, and heat up your film. If you plan to be on an open boat for several hours, be sure to cover your camera with a wet towel and keep it in the shade.

Rinse and soak your camera after every dive: A quick rinse or dunk does not get all the saltwater off your camera or housing, especially when it comes to those hard-to-reach spots under knobs and dials. When you're on a dive boat, be sure to soak your camera in the freshwater "dunk bucket" for at least fifteen minutes. If you do have access to a sink, tub, or dunk bucket, it's a good idea to soak your camera overnight.

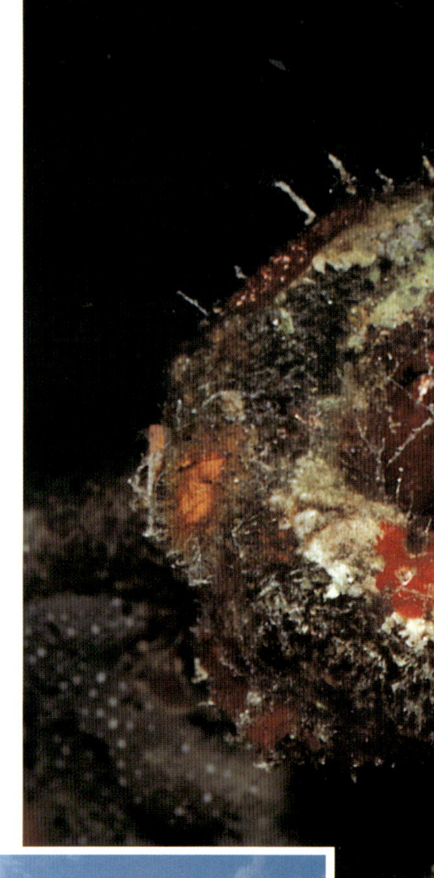

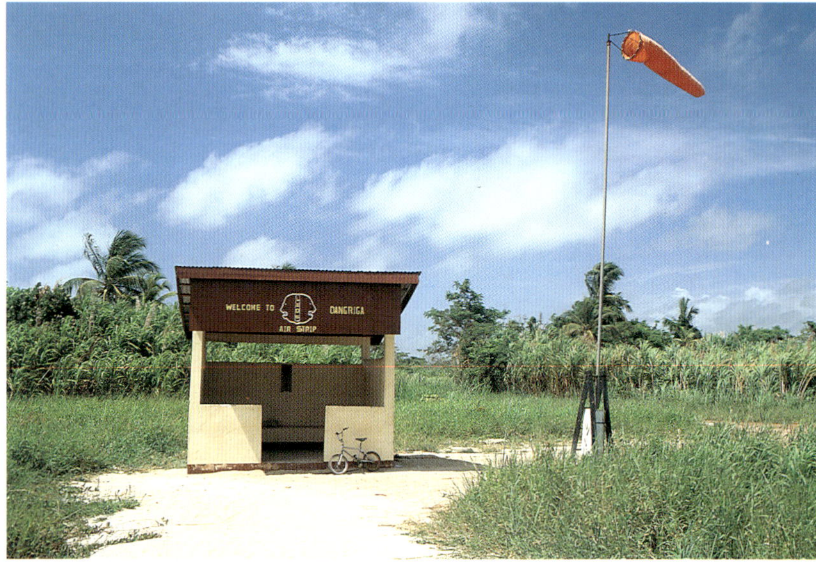

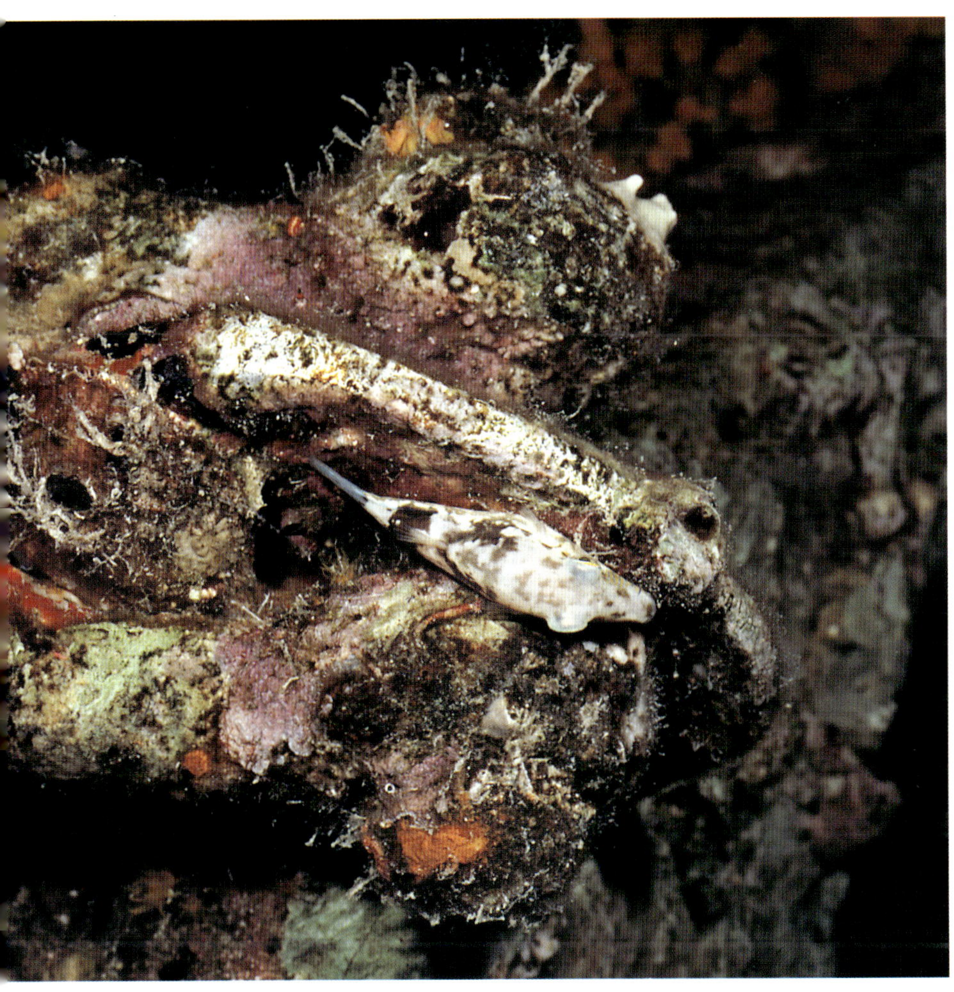

ABOVE: By reading about the underwater environment, you'll develop an eye for small, hard-to-see underwater creatures, like this small sharpnose pufferfish hiding on a coral-encrusted docking ring of a shipwreck. (See suggested books, page 119.) **Subject:** Sharpnose pufferfish. **Site:** Bonaire, Netherlands Antilles. **Equipment and film:** Nikonos RS, 50mm lens, Nikonos SB-104 strobe, Kodak Elite 100. OPPOSITE: If you plan to travel to remote locations, bring all your camera cleaning gear with you. O-ring grease and spare O-rings are not common items in the tropics—like at this airport in southern Belize, Central America.

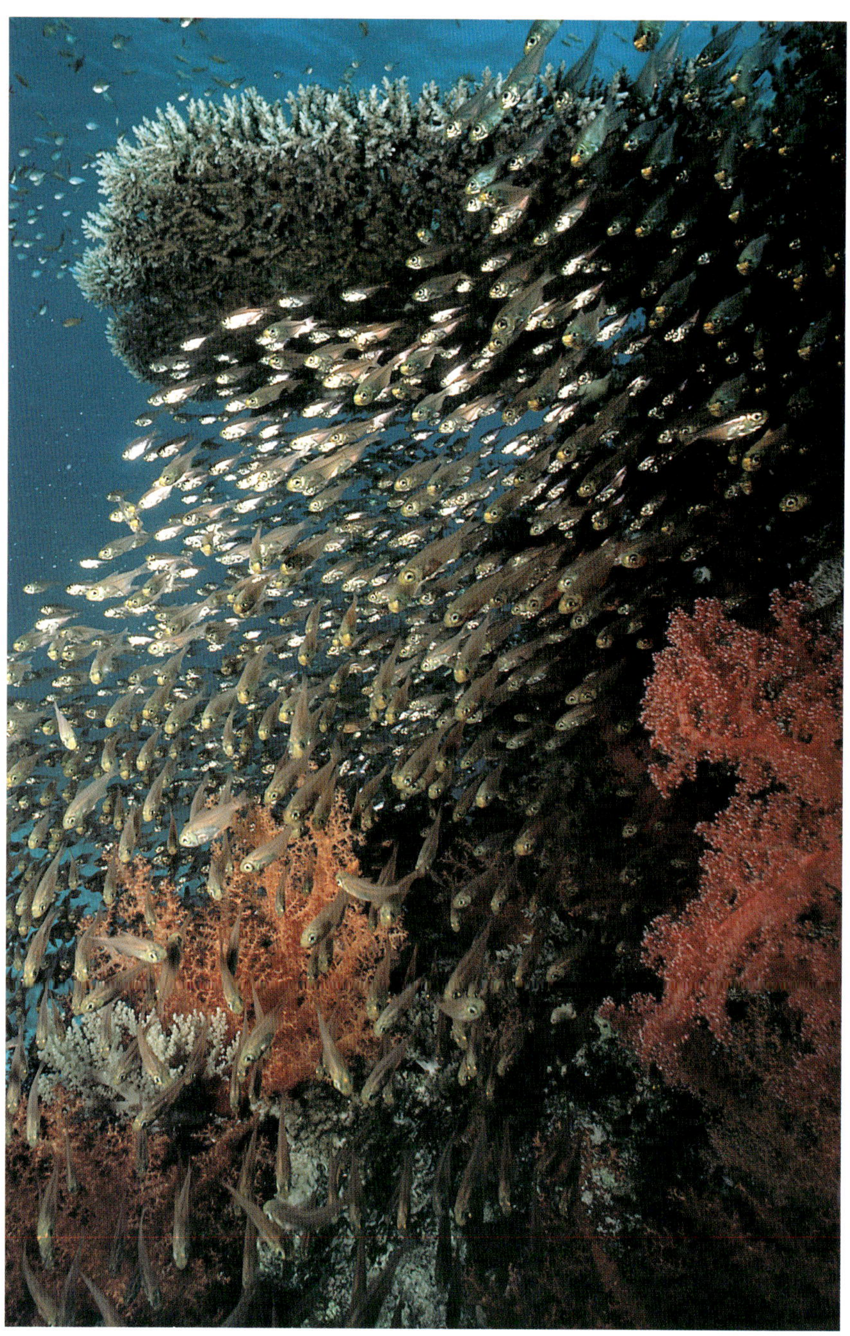

Nothing captures the color, beauty, and wonder of the coral reef like a wide-angle photograph. Here, two strobes were used for even lighting over the entire frame. **Subject:** Silversides on coral head. **Site:** Northern Red Sea, Egypt. **Equipment and film:** Nikonos V, Sea & Sea 15mm lens, two Nikonos SB-103 strobes, Kodachrome 64.

Chapter 9: Capturing the Wide View—Naturally and with a Strobe

The best ways to capture those compelling seascapes and fascinating shipwrecks on film.

Even though I've been diving for more than fourteen years, I'm often overwhelmed by underwater panoramic views—sprawling coral gardens and breathtaking walls that create multicolored seascapes. If you've been diving for a while, you know what I'm talking about. If you are new to scuba diving, you're in for a treat!

Capturing the beauty of underwater seascapes, as well as wide-angle views of shipwrecks, is the focus of this chapter. (For more discussion on composition in general, see also "The Basics.")

Lenses: I recommend 15mm to 24mm wide-angle lenses for photographing reefs and shipwrecks, for three reasons. First, they let you shoot close to subjects. The closer you get, the sharper your pictures will be. Second, these lenses "see" large areas of a reef or wreck, conveying the beauty and scale of the site. Third, 15mm to 24mm lenses offer good depth of field, so you get more subjects in focus in your photographs.

When choosing and using a wide-angle lens, remember: The wider the angle, the more you will get in your picture and the more you'll get in focus. In the equipment chapter, you'll find a complete list of the wide-angle lenses that are available for underwater cameras and for autofocus SLR cameras that can be used in underwater housings.

With wide-angle lenses (and all lenses for that matter), it's important to note the *f*-stop at which you are shooting. Since you want to get as much in focus as possible, shoot at the smallest *f*-stop possible for the existing lighting condition.

When shooting wide, you can shoot either natural light pictures or flash

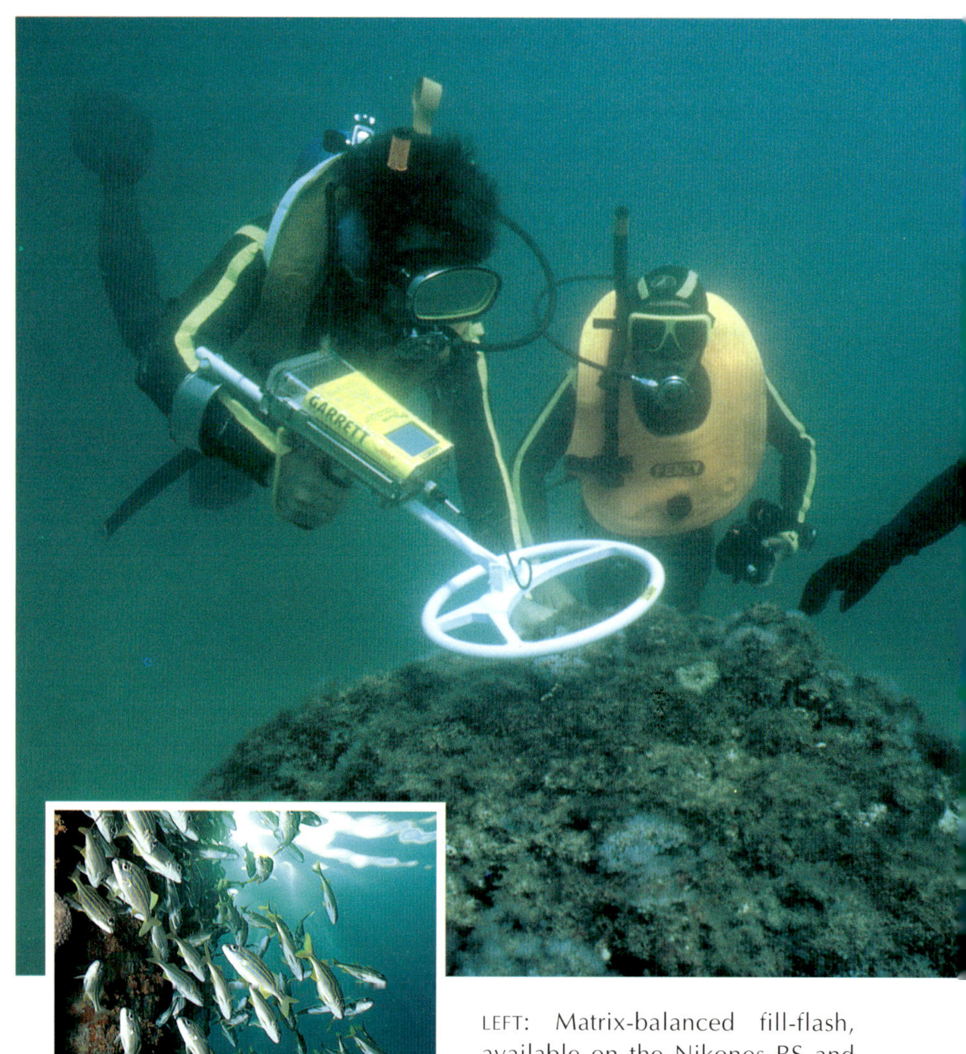

LEFT: Matrix-balanced fill-flash, available on the Nikonos RS and Nikonos 8008s, take all the guesswork out of getting balanced daylight-to-flash pictures. **Subject:** Yellow tails. **Site:** Bonaire Town Pier, Netherlands Antilles. **Equipment and film:** Nikonos V, 15mm lens, Nikonos SB-104 strobe, Kodak Elite 100.

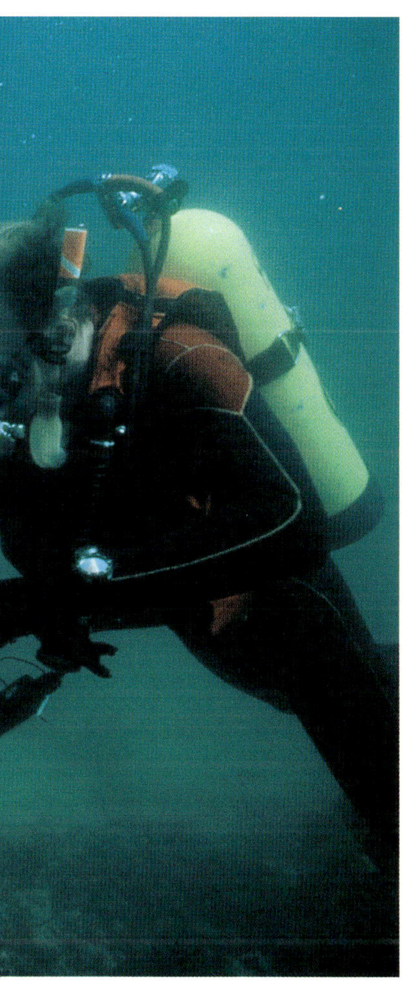

pictures. Because natural light pictures are relatively easy to take, let's take a look at these techniques first.

Wide-Angle Natural Light Pictures

Film: When taking wide-angle natural light pictures under water, film type is especially important. By choosing the most appropriate film for your diving depth, you will be able to get the best color possible and "freeze" the movement of fast-swimming subjects.

As a general guideline, when shooting above thirty feet, ISO 50 to 100 film is a good choice. When you dive deeper, switch to ISO 400 or 800 film.

Natural light exposures: Because wide-angle lenses take in a wide area, getting a correct automatic exposure requires careful framing and attention to your camera controls. Here's why: Unless you want a mood shot or a silhouette, you need as little contrast in the scene as possible. Otherwise, the highlights may be washed out or the shadow areas may become black. For example, if you are photographing a reef wall at sunrise and are shooting toward the sun, framing the scene with both the underwater sunburst and reef in your picture may cause the reef to be underexposed, with little or no detail. This happens because the bright light from the sun can "fool" the camera's light meter into "thinking" the scene is actually brighter than it is, resulting in an underexposed reef. In this situation, you would be better off framing the scene so that the reef and a dark section of the water fill the frame.

When taking wide-angle pictures of divers or large fish with your camera set on "A" (automatic), shooting with the sun at your back will produce an evenly illuminated subject. When you shoot with your subject between you and an underwater sunburst, you can get a silhouette. You can also get nice silhouettes of elkhorn coral formations and ships' masts with a wide-angle lens when your camera is set on "A" and you're shooting toward the sun.

You can fine-tune your natural light exposures by using the "M" (manual) mode. When shooting slide film, meter the brightest portion of the scene in the "A" mode and note the *f*-stop and shutter speed. Then, switch to the "M" mode without changing the *f*-stop or shutter speed. Now, recompose your scene and shoot. By following this method, the brightest portion of the scene will be correctly exposed.

If you don't meter the brightest area of a scene when using slide film, the highlights in your picture may be washed out, ruining your image. Exposure of slide film must be quite precise for optimum results.

When shooting print film, meter the darkest portion of the scene in the "A" mode and follow the procedure mentioned above for a pleasing exposure. Why meter the darker area? Print film has a wide exposure latitude and can handle wide contrast scenes (to a point). By metering the darker area and setting your exposure accordingly, you will not lose shadow detail, and your highlights will probably not be washed out. (See also the chapter "Choosing the Right Film.")

Shooting shallow: Wide-angle, natural light photos taken in shallow water can be impressive, especially if your subject is a whale shark or a shipwreck. In fact, when photographing these subjects from a distance, natural light is the only way to go.

Wide-Angle Flash Pictures

In the early days of underwater photography, getting good flash pictures was a bit tricky. However, with today's sophisticated cameras and flash units, it's relatively easy to get good flash pictures if you know the basics.

Automatic exposure pictures: There's an old saying among photography teachers: "The name of the game is to fill the frame." This means that if you fill the frame with the subject, you'll have a pretty good chance of getting a good flash exposure. For example, if you fill the frame with a clownfish surrounded by the tentacles of a sea anemone, the flash will evenly illuminate both the fish and the anemone, so your exposure should be right on. However, if you take an automatic flash picture of a fish in open water, the surrounding water will not reflect light back to the camera's TTL (through-the-lens) light sensor, fooling the camera's meter into thinking that the scene is darker than it actually is. The result would probably be an overexposed picture.

To remedy this situation, either move in closer to fill the frame with the subject or, if you have a +/- exposure compensation dial on your camera, set the dial to -1, thus reducing the amount of light from the strobe reaching your subject. If you have time, take an additional exposure at -2, which further reduces the light output. It's a good idea to make two exposures because different fish reflect light differently, some more than others. Also, the correct exposure depends on how much of the frame your subject fills.

When using a TTL camera and automatic strobe, you can reduce the light output from the strobe by adjusting your camera's ISO dial. If you are using ISO 100 film, set the ISO dial at 200. Technically, this reduces the light output from the strobe by one stop.

When shooting with a fully automatic camera and automatic strobe, there's another technique to get a properly exposed flash picture of a fish surrounded by lots of blue water. Here's the trick. Most automatic strobes have a flash confirmation light that indicates the "correct" exposure— correct, that is, if the subject fills most of the frame. When the subject does not fill the frame, simply move the strobe away from the subject and shoot a few frames until the light blinks rapidly, indicating a "technically" under-exposed picture. In reality, you should get a correctly exposed picture.

Very reflective fish can also fool a camera's light meter. For example, when taking a flash picture of a barracuda or other silver-sided fish, the strobe light reflecting back through the lens may turn off the strobe too soon, resulting in an underexposed picture or a picture with a hot spot (a bright reflection of light in one area rather than balanced light over the whole subject). As mentioned above, when shooting with a flash in the "A" mode, filling the frame will compensate somewhat for this imbalance in contrast.

Manual exposure flash pictures: In many cases, you'll get a properly exposed subject when you shoot on automatic. However, when photographing very bright or very dark subjects, manual exposure may be preferred.

When shooting in the manual mode, select the recommended flash sync speed on your camera (see your instruction manual) and set your strobe for manual operation. Then, determine the flash-to-subject distance (which may be different than the camera-to-subject distance), check the recommended *f*-stop on the aperture/subject distance chart (which should be attached to your strobe), set your lens accordingly, and shoot. If you have time, make additional exposures one *f*-stop over and one *f*-stop under that setting.

When shooting with slide film, it's also a good idea to bracket your flash exposures in half or quarter stops. Naturally, shooting on automatic is faster and easier than shooting on manual. However, if you have time to set up a shot, shooting on manual may produce better results.

Daylight-balanced, fill-flash pictures: For me the key to a good daylight, wide-angle, underwater flash picture is to make it look like a natural light picture—that is, one that was not taken with a strobe or strobes. There are fairly complicated flash calculation charts to help you determine how to do this. However, with today's automatic cameras, it's relatively simple. For example, if you own a Nikonos V, set the camera on "A" and adjust the *f*-stop until both the 1/125 and 1/60 lights are illuminated on the shutter speed scale in the viewfinder. This means that the camera is set at shutter speed of 1/90 second—the automatic sync speed. Now set your Nikonos strobe on TTL. If your subject is within flash range (you can check this on the flash-to-subject distance scale on your strobe), you will most likely get a very natural-looking picture.

Backscatter: Amateur and professional underwater photographers the world over have a common enemy: backscatter. Backscatter, which is most prevalent in wide-angle pictures, is the result of the light from the strobe reflecting off the ever-present particles in the water and into the lens. The resulting effect in a picture looks like an underwater snowstorm. In most cases, backscatter can ruin a picture.

Backscatter can be reduced, and even eliminated, by placing or holding the strobe off-camera. This causes the light to bounce off the particles at an angle and not directly into the lens.

Holding or positioning the strobe off-camera not only helps to reduce backscatter, but also offers different creative lighting possibilities, such as top-, side-, front-, and perhaps even backlighting. If you see a subject you want to capture on film, experiment with different strobe positions. Who knows? You may be pleasantly surprised at the shadows and highlights produced by varying the strobe position.

Before we move on to the next chapter, remember the three underwater flash photography tips that may prove invaluable on your next dive trip:

❋ Attach your flash diffuser to your strobe with fishing line or light string so it does not twist off and float away, which can easily happen if it's not securely attached;

❋ Bring an extra sync cord or two, just in case of a malfunction or a leak, which can short-circuit your wiring;

❋ Check all of the following: batteries to see that they are installed correctly, O-rings to make sure they are clean and greased, sync connections to make sure they are secure, and the tray screw to make sure your camera and strobe are firmly in place.

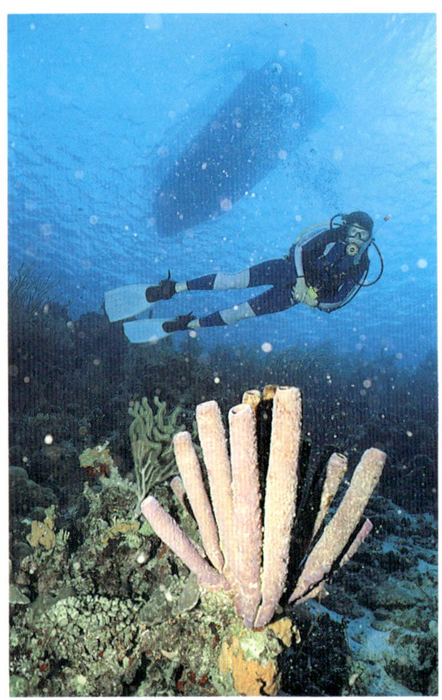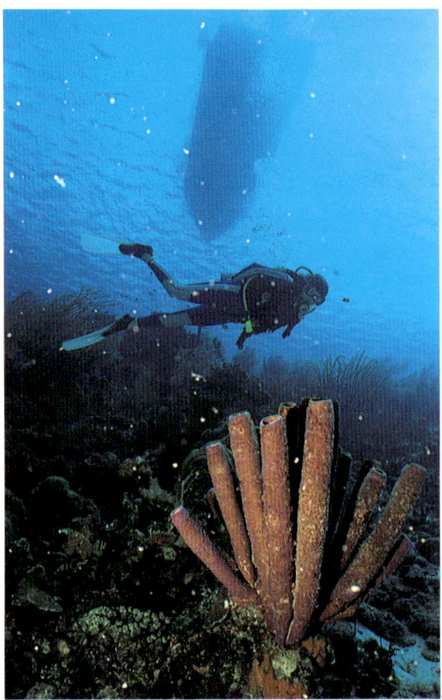

ABOVE AND OPPOSITE: Wide-angle underwater photography is especially challenging because wide-angle lenses can take in expansive scenes in which subjects are on different planes. This may cause at least one subject to be overexposed (ABOVE LEFT). Another problem is light reflecting at an unwanted angle off of back-scatter, which is caused by having the strobe too close to the lens (ABOVE RIGHT). However, with careful metering, bracketing, subject placement, and composition, wide-angle shots can't be beat to capture the beauty beneath the surface (OPPOSITE). **Subject:** Tube sponges, diver, dive boat. **Site:** Bonaire, Netherlands Antilles. **Equipment and film:** Nikonos V, 15mm lens, Nikonos SB-104 strobe, Kodak Elite 100.

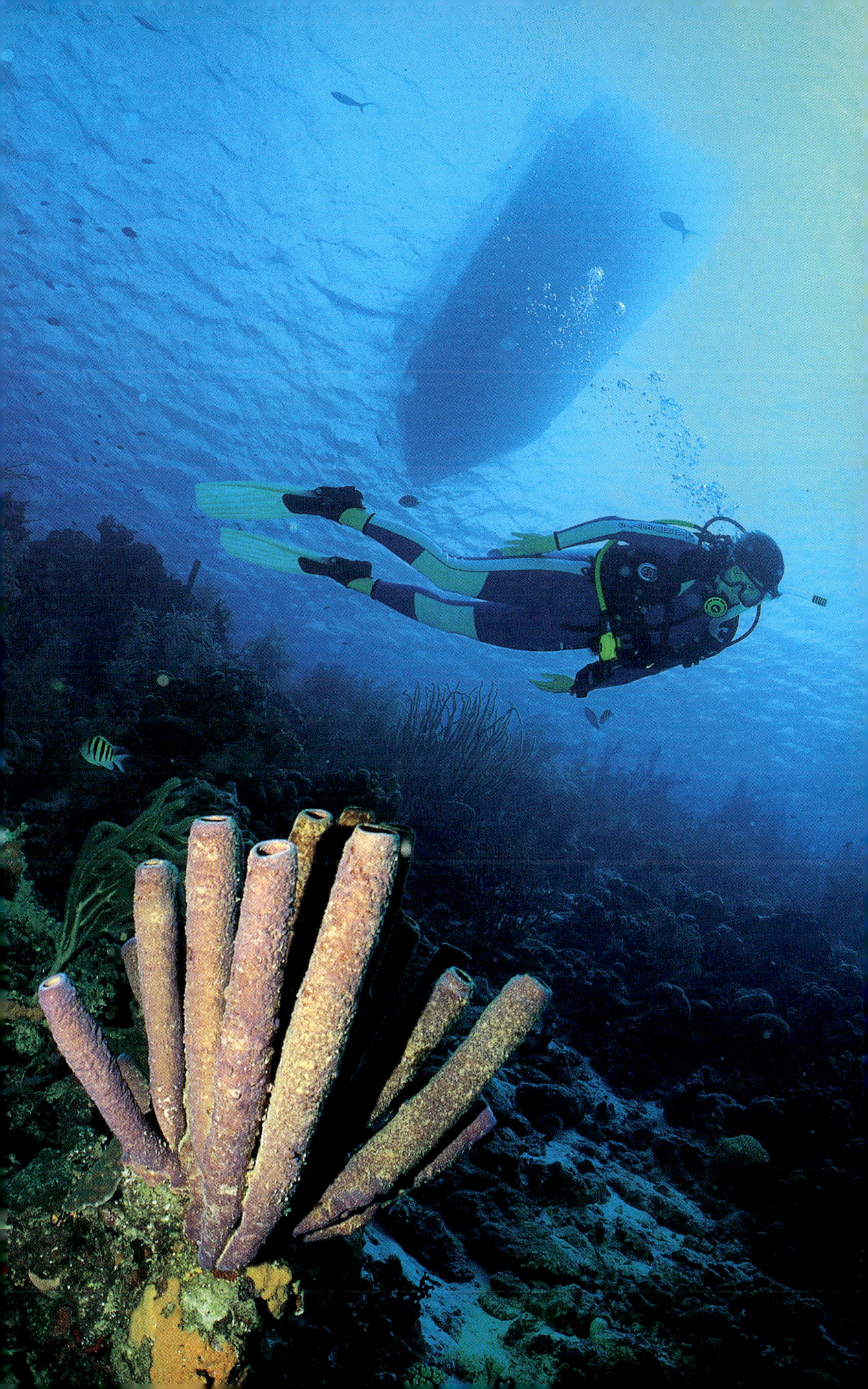

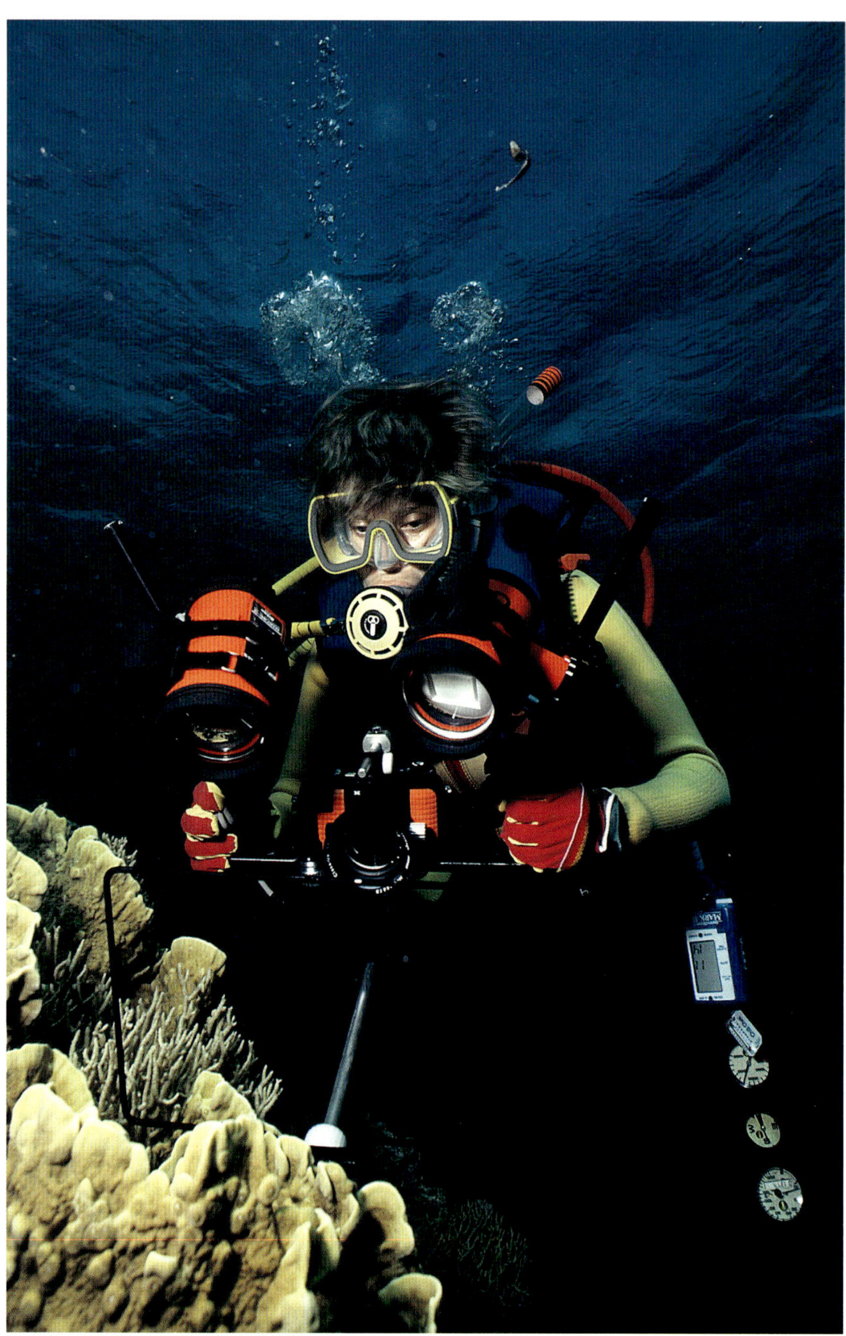

Wire framers that attach to underwater cameras make taking macro pictures easy. Simply position the framer around the subject and shoot. This diver is using two strobes for shadowless lighting.

Chapter 10: Shooting Close-ups—Day and Night

Techniques for shooting super-sharp, bursting-with-color close-ups.

Sea water limits our underwater long-distance vision and the clarity of our wide-angle pictures. In the relatively dense water column, countless microscopic animals—zooplankton and phytoplankton—float among silt, sand, and sediment, reducing visibility.

In this environment, we often see a coral reef in soft-focus, where shapes and patterns are muted. So how does one get super-sharp underwater pictures that "pop" with color and detail? By shooting as close as possible to the subject. In other words, by utilizing macro equipment and close-up techniques.

In many ways, shooting close-ups is easier than shooting standard wide-angle photographs. Still, there are certain things you need to know if you want to get the best possible close-up photographs.

Two things are a "must." First, you need to shoot at the smallest f-stop possible, for maximum depth of field. Second, you must shoot with a strobe, because shooting under water at small f-stops requires artificial lighting to ensure proper exposure. A strobe will also bring out the fabulous colors and details of marine life.

With these thoughts in mind, here's a look at some of the options available for close-up photography. (For more discussion on composition in general, see also "The Basics.")

Film: If you like slides, you'll want to shoot with a slow film, such as Kodachrome 25, Kodachrome 64, or Ektachrome Underwater 50. If prints are your preference, you may want to try Kodak's Royal Gold 100. These relatively slow films have a fine grain. By reducing the amount of grain in your pictures, you increase apparent sharpness.

A slow film will be sufficient in most situations. However, there are two cases when you may need a higher speed film in order to shoot at a small *f*-stop. The first is when shooting with high-magnification extension tubes, which increase the distance light has to travel from the front element of the lens to the film plane. The second is when shooting with an SLR lens and the subject is more than a few inches from your camera, which also increases the distance the light has to travel. In these close-up situations, Ektachrome 100 or Fujichrome 100 for slides, or Kodak Royal Gold 100 or Fujicolor 100 for prints, will let you shoot at small *f*-stops.

To determine which film is best for your system, experiment with different films at home before you go on vacation. You can experiment in a pool or bathtub, which will produce virtually the same close-up results as you'll get under water. However, in-air photos taken with extension tubes and close-up kits will show the wire framers in your test shots. This happens because extension tubes and close-up kits are designed to compensate for refraction, which changes the field of view under water. (See also the chapter "Choosing the Right Film.")

Autofocus macro lenses: Autofocus SLR camera owners can shoot with a 60mm or 105mm macro lens in underwater camera housings. (These are the focal lengths of Nikon's macro lenses. Other camera manufacturers' focal lengths may vary.)

My standard close-up lens is a 60mm macro lens. I like this lens because it lets me photograph everything from a quarter-inch-long shrimp to a foot-long grouper. However, I need to be relatively close when using this lens—which can intimidate some fishes and invertebrates. When I need to shoot small, shy subjects, I use a 105mm macro lens, which provides a slightly greater camera-to-subject distance than the 60mm lens.

Close-up attachments: Whether you own a Nikonos V or a Sea & Sea Seamaster Pro, close-up attachments will increase your camera's versatil-

OPPOSITE: Close-up photography does not necessarily mean shooting with a macro lens. In this sequence, the first photo (TOP) was taken with a zoom lens set at 20mm, and the second (MIDDLE) was taken with the same lens set at 35mm. The third photo (BOTTOM) was also taken with the lens set at the 35mm setting, but this time I moved in for a tight head shot. **Subject:** Giant sea turtle, sleeping. **Site:** South Africa. **Equipment and film:** Nikon N8008s, Stromm One underwater housing, 20–35mm zoom lens, Nikonos SB-104 strobe, Fujichrome 100.

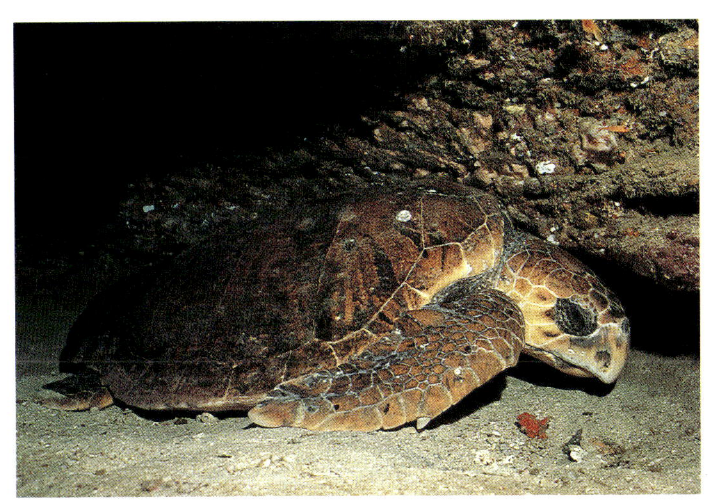
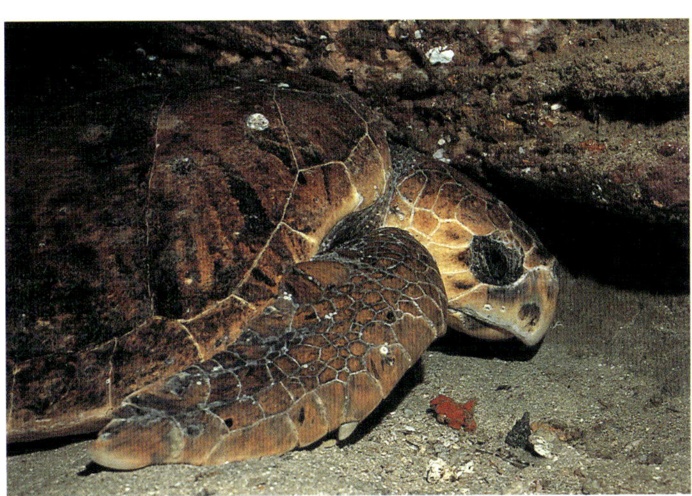
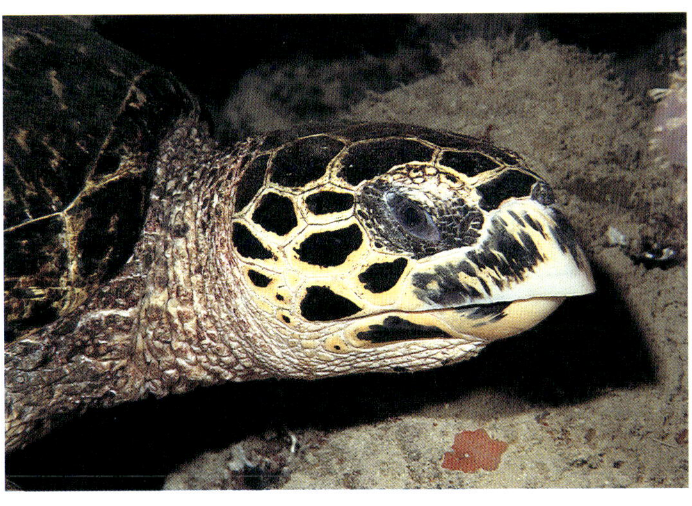

ity and your personal enjoyment in taking underwater pictures. (You don't need close-up attachments for the Nikonos RS because a true macro lens is available.) Close-up attachments consist of a lens—or an extension tube that attaches to your lens—and a wire framer in which you position your subject. The lens is usually a 28mm or 35mm focal length. The advantage to using a framer is that you simply move the framer around the subject and shoot. This is great for photographing corals, small invertebrates, and sleeping fish. However, the framer does scare most fishes away. So, if you want lots of close-ups of fishes, a macro lens on an SLR in a housing is the way to go.

Both the Nikonos V Close-up Kit (for the Nikonos 28mm, 35mm, and 80mm lenses) and the Sea & Sea Macro Lenses (1:3 and 1:2) can be attached and removed under water, giving you increased shooting possibilities. Extension tubes, available in magnifications from half life-size to larger than life-size, fit between the lens and the camera body (so, obviously, you can't do a quick change under water).

Because the Nikonos Close-up Kit and most extension tubes are sold in sets, you'll have an opportunity to experiment with different magnifications. For example, the Nikonos 28mm lens with the Close-up Kit is ideal for photographing sleeping butterflyfish and parrotfish, while a 1:1 extension tube will give you a nice full-frame picture of a Christmas tree worm.

One important point to remember when shooting with close-up kits and extension tubes is that they make your camera more vulnerable to flooding, especially on a night dive when it is considerably easier to bump into something. The apparatus on the front lens puts increased pressure on the O-ring seal. If you accidentally knock into a coral head or rest your camera on the framer on the deck of your dive boat, you can twist the lens and cause an ever-so-small opening between the lens and camera body that could result in a not-so-small repair bill.

Wide-angle close-ups: Don't overlook the possibilities of wide-angle close-up photos on night dives. Wide-angle pictures have much more depth of field than pictures taken with close-up accessories. For example, when set at *f/22* and the minimum focusing distance, the Nikonos 15mm lens offers a depth of field of about six inches to three feet. When the Nikonos Close-up Kit is used on a 28mm lens, the depth of field is only a few inches.

Strobes: Fine art photographers consider their art "painting with light." In

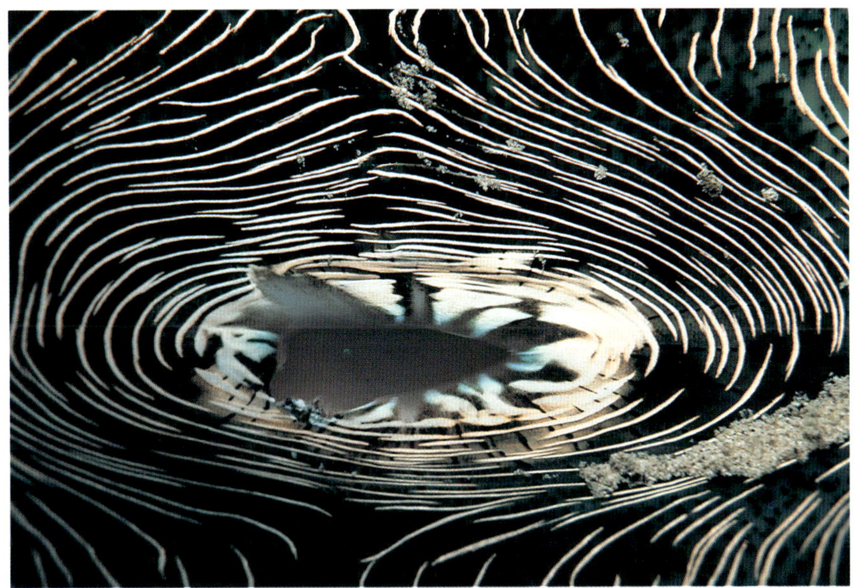

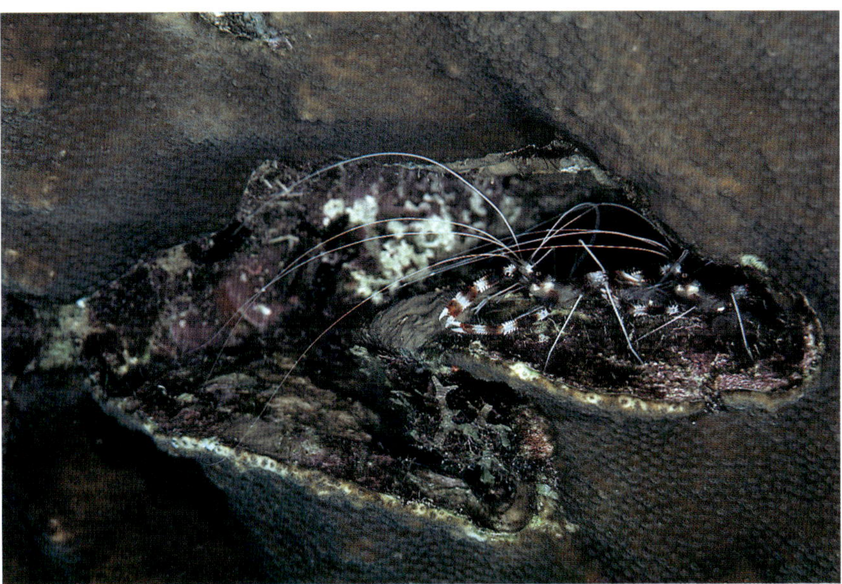

TOP: Close-ups of stationary subjects can be taken with close-up attachments, which have framers in which you frame the subject. Close-up attachments are not recommended for photographing fish (unless they are sleeping) because it's almost impossible to get the fish in the frame. ABOVE: Dual strobes offer shadowless lighting. **Subject:** Banded coral shrimps. **Site:** Bonaire, Netherlands Antilles. **Equipment and film:** Nikon 8008s, Stromm One underwater housing, 60mm lens, two Nikonos SB-103 strobes, Kodak Elite 100.

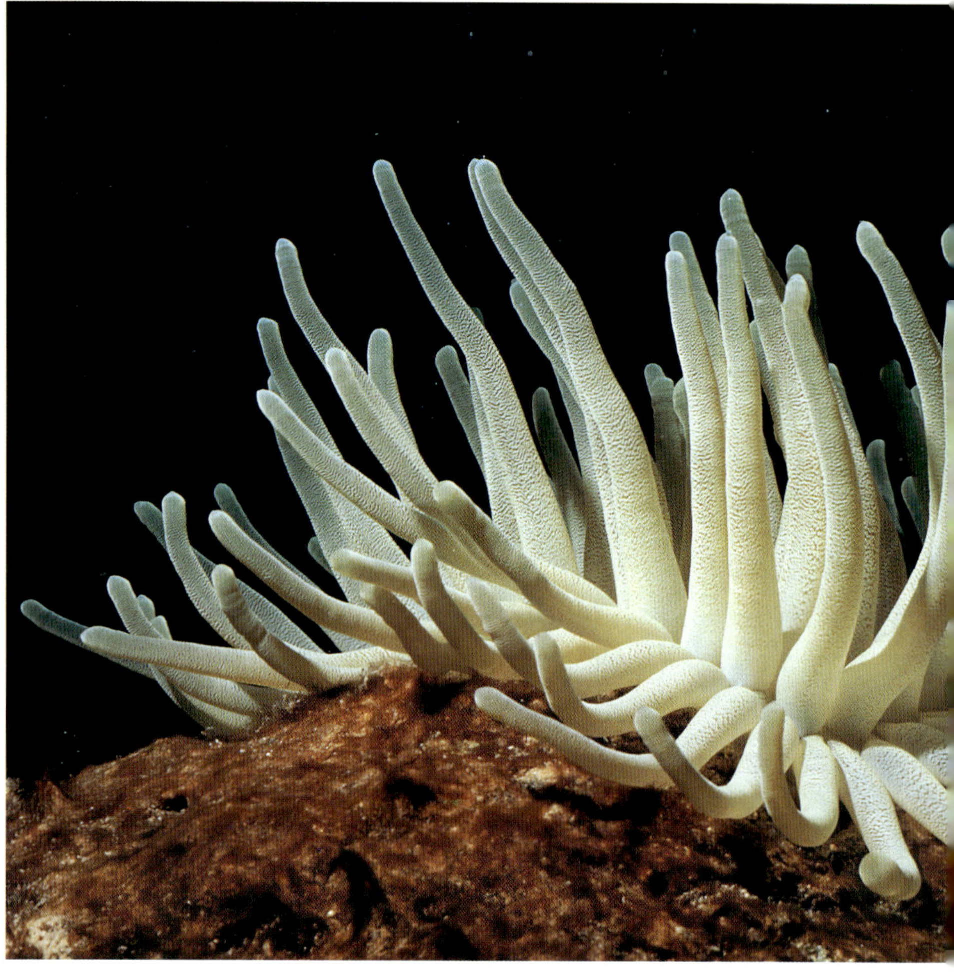

When the background will distract from the main subject, hold the flash directly over the subject so that no light falls on the background elements. **Subject:** Sea anemone. **Site:** Bonaire, Netherlands Antilles. **Equipment and film:** Nikonos RS, 50mm lens, Nikonos SB-104 strobe, Kodak Elite 100.

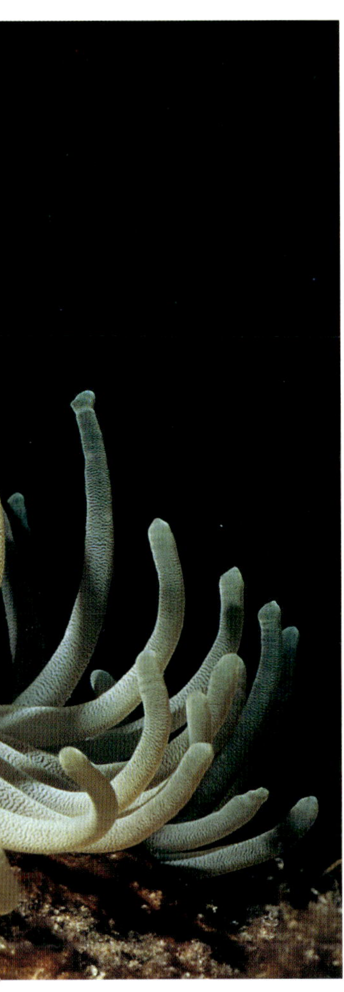

fact, this is what a photographer does when he or she lights a subject to the desirable illumination, creates a dramatic shadow or highlights areas, and exposes a frame of film. In underwater macro photography, where you are working close to your subject, you have a variety of lighting possibilities.

With a single strobe, for example, you can position the strobe unit over, to the left or right, or even behind your subject. On TTL, you'll get a proper exposure most of the time. However, for additional creative effects, you may want to set the strobe on manual and vary the distance from the subject. In any event, when shooting with a single strobe, do what famed National Geographic photographer David Doubilet recommends: "Take the damn strobe off the camera."

After you experiment with one strobe, you really should see what two strobes can do. Dual-strobe lighting offers two advantages. First, it provides more light so you can shoot at a smaller *f*-stop for more depth of field (highly desirable in close-up photography). Second, it offers more creative possibilities, such as producing shadowless lighting and ratio lighting, in which you can have one strobe set at full for your main light source and have the other set at one-fourth power for just a touch of fill light.

Exposure: By now you can see that setting your strobe on TTL will deliver a good exposure in most situations. To ensure a proper exposure, bracket each image by shooting one stop over and one stop under the recommended setting.

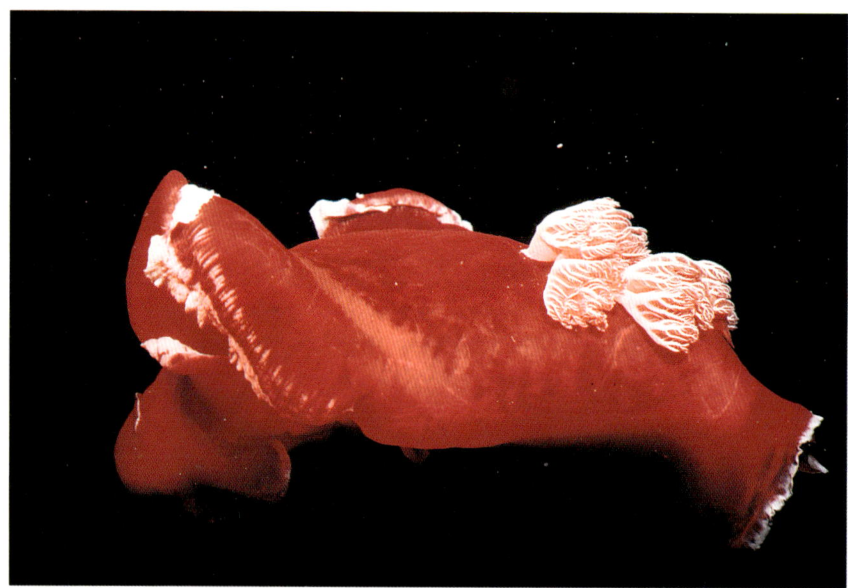

Diving at night reveals the wonders of the moonlit reef. When shooting open-water subjects with a black background, fill the frame with the subject to avoid an incorrect through-the-lens flash meter reading. **Subject:** Spanish dancer. **Site:** Red Sea, Egypt. **Equipment and film;** Nikonos V, 28mm lens, Close-up Kit, Nikonos SB-103 strobe, Kodachrome 64.

Chapter 11: Shooting in the Dark

When and where to dive, and finding nocturnal fish and invertebrates.

Night dives are as different from day dives as, well, night and day, but close-up photography techniques are identical. However, there are differences in the animals you see on the reef at night and in how you'll spot your subject.

Before we get to some pointers on night diving, I must tell you this: I love night diving. For me, there are few things more thrilling than sitting on a dive boat at night, strapping on a tank, slipping over the side of the boat into total blackness, and slowly watching the reef come into view in the beam of my dive light.

In the darkness of night, the reef becomes the domain of nocturnal fishes and invertebrates and predators in search of a meal. Most diurnal fishes are safely tucked away in the nooks and crannies of the reef, and others are asleep on the reef itself. But perhaps what makes night diving special are the incredible colors. Once the sun has set, the delicate and colorful polyps of the hard corals are in full bloom, adding even more color to an already resplendent reef.

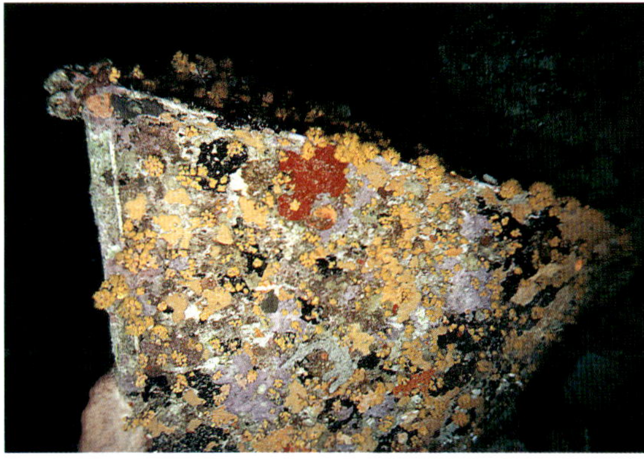

Wide-angle close-ups taken at night are especially dramatic, particularly when the subject is bursting with color. **Subject:** Sunken rowboat. **Site:** Bonaire, Netherlands Antilles. **Equipment and film:** Nikonos RS, 20–35mm zoom lens set at 20mm, Nikonos SB-104 strobe, Kodak Elite 100.

If you want to experience the thrill of night diving, here are a few things to consider.

When to dive: For the beginner, it's a good idea to dive shallow (about thirty to forty feet) and enter the water just after the sun has set, when there still are traces of natural light on the reef. Diving at twilight gives you a good idea of the layout of the reef before the scene turns to darkness, eliminating any apprehension you may have about entering unknown territory.

The later the night dive, however, the more fishes you'll see asleep on and in the reef, and the more crabs and shrimps you'll find staring at you from the relative safety of small caves and overhangs. In some locations, darkness brings some fishes to the surface to feed on plankton. In others, night brings sharks, manta rays, and other large marine creatures to inshore reefs.

Dive light: One of the most essential pieces of equipment for the night diver is a good, dependable dive light, complete with fresh batteries that have recently been tested. On moonless nights, a diver without a light is blind under water.

Most night divers carry two lights: a main light and a dependable spare. Some divers also carry a chemical light stick just in case both lights malfunction (see "What to Bring on Your Dive Trip—Essential Accessories"). The light stick can't be used for seeing under water, but it's a bright beacon that a dive boat can follow in an emergency.

Photographers who shoot at night usually mount their dive lights directly on their underwater strobes using rubber holsters, which are sold at dive shops. This mounting technique serves two purposes. First, it frees up the diver's hands. Second, when the dive light illuminates the subject, the strobe light automatically will be aimed in the right direction. Underwater photographers who dive with dual-strobe systems sometimes mount a light on each strobe, giving them good visibility under water as well as an accurate method for aiming both strobes.

One final note on night diving (and all diving for that matter): Never dive alone. Always write up a detailed plan of your dive with your buddy and then dive your plan. A buddy is there to help you out of a potential jam and vice versa. In addition, his or her eyes will help you find twice the number of tiny, interesting reef creatures to photograph.

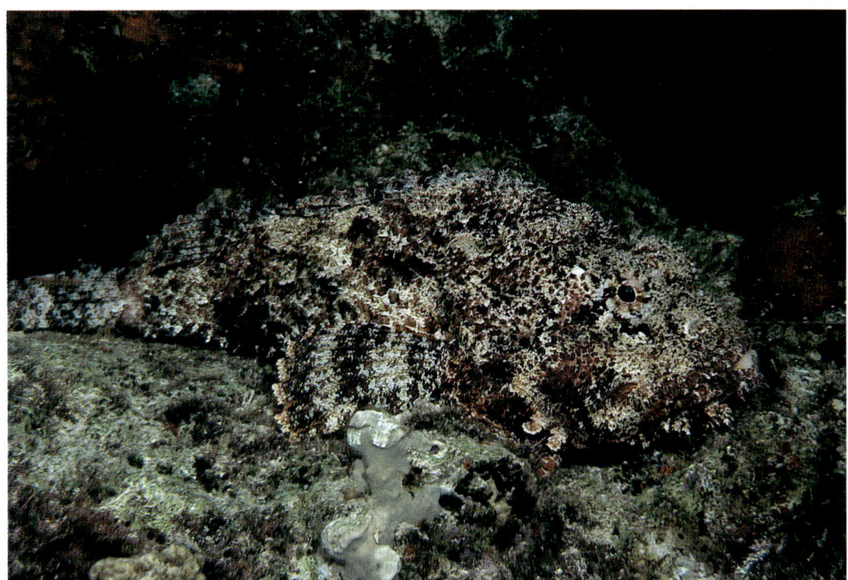

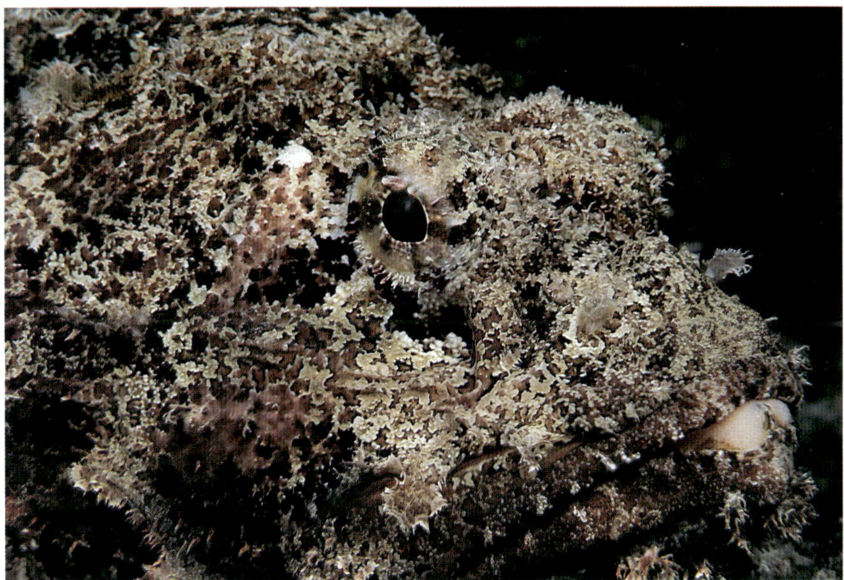

TOP AND ABOVE: If you want full-frame, close-up pictures of fish, dive at night—when many reef fish are sleeping. In some cases, you can get within inches of the fish before it wakes up or gets startled. **Subject (both photos):** Scorpionfish. **Site:** Bonaire, Netherlands Antilles. **Equipment and film:** Nikonos RS, 50mm lens, two Nikonos SB-103 strobes, Kodak Elite 100.

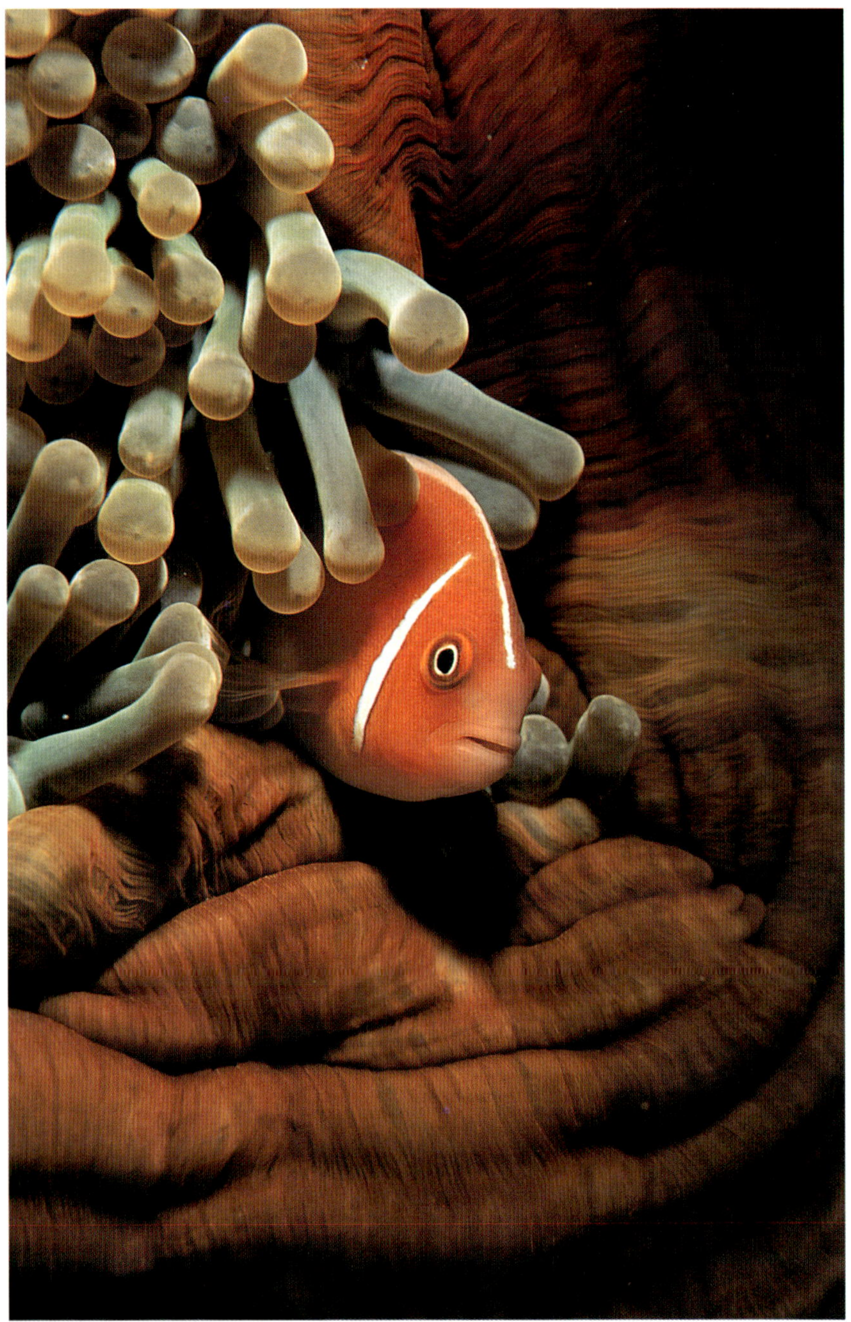

Following basic rules—such as "The name of the game is to fill the frame"—will help you get great shots, even on your first dive. But remember: Breaking the rules on subsequent photographic adventures will result in inventive shots. **Subject:** Clownfish in a sea anemone. **Site:** Fiji Islands, South Pacific. **Equipment and film:** Nikon 8008s, Stromm One underwater housing, 60mm lens, Nikonos SB-103 strobe, Kodachrome 64.

Chapter 12: Breaking the Rules

Composition, lighting, film choice, and exposure guidelines, once mastered, are meant to be broken.

Now that you know "all" the rules of photography, I need to tell you this: Rules are meant to be broken.

To illustrate this point, I'd like to share with you the "photo philosophy" of a friend of mine, noted professional photographer Robert Huntzinger. Huntzinger says "It's often amateur photographers who lead the way in creative photography because they don't have to follow all the so-called rules of photography for composition, lighting, exposure and so on.

"I believe a novice photographer is somewhat like being a child," Huntzinger continues. "Often, children are forgiven for 'not knowing any better.' Well, amateurs often 'don't know any better,' but they do come up with unusual photographs, some of which can be prize winners. When the rules are not followed, we get to see new and fresh approaches to photographing commonplace subjects."

With Huntzinger's photo philosophy in mind, I'd like to encourage you to break the rules—after your have mastered them. Don't get caught up in the technology of picture-taking. Rather, concentrate on your subject or the scene and try to capture it as you see it and not how you may have seen it pictured in a dive magazine, or even in this book.

To help you start "breaking the rules":

❀ Experiment with shutter speeds—see how they can freeze or blur motion;

❀ Try framing the same scene in several different ways. Learn how just the slightest change in camera position can make the difference between a snapshot and a great shot;

❀ After you have found the finest grain film, experiment with fast films to see how grain can enhance a picture;

❀ When shooting with a strobe, try different strobe positions, behind and above the subject;

❀ Don't always fill the frame with your subject, though even I often follow this rule. Look through your camera's viewfinder and see how "dead space" (open water) can enhance a reef scene or a picture of a school of fish.

Finally, think about something else Huntzinger once said to me. When discussing "good" versus "bad" pictures, he encourages photographers to remember that there are no right shots and no wrong shots. He feels that each shot is different, and each expresses how an individual sees a particular situation. "In my mind," he says, "a good photograph is about what the individual feels is a good photograph. It reflects the photographer's energy for photography."

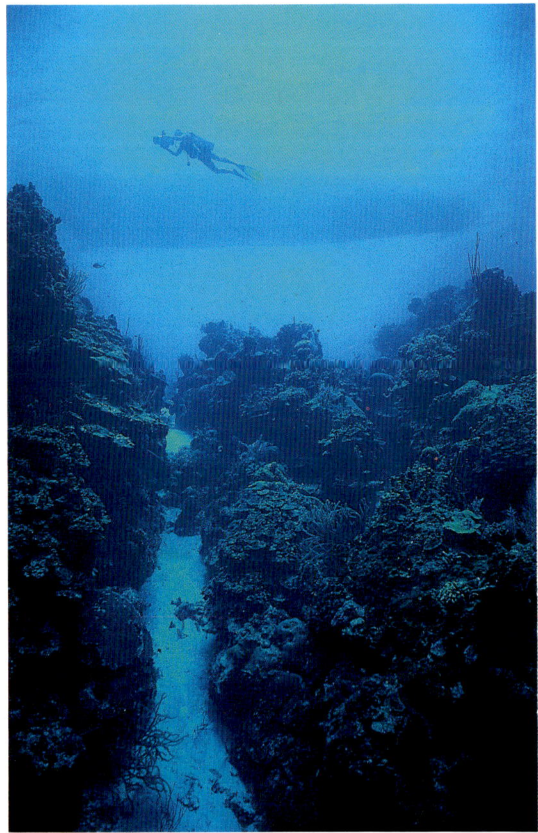

Most underwater photographers would not take a photo that encompasses such a large scene as this, especially with the lack of color and detail in the image. However, for me it brings back the memory of a great dive. And, from a scientific standpoint, it illustrates the spur-and-groove reef formation. **Subject:** Barrier reef. **Site:** Belize, Central America. **Equipment and film:** Sea & Sea Motor Marine II, 20mm lens, Fujichrome 100.

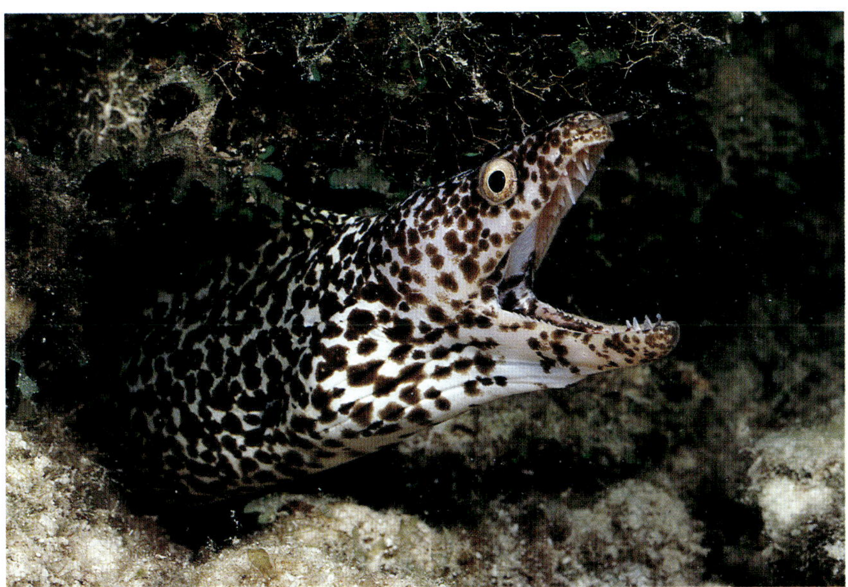

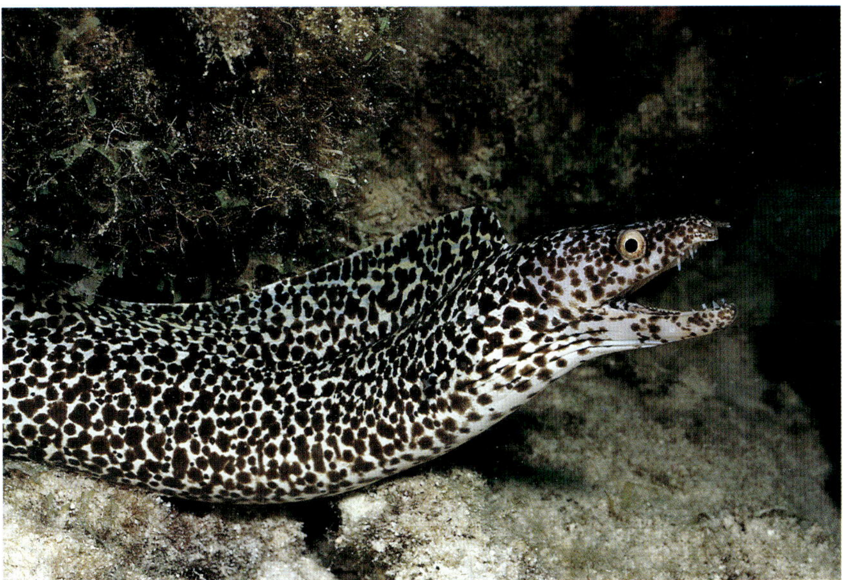

In underwater photography, there are no right or wrong shots. Rather, there are pictures that some photographers like better than others. In this set, the first photo (TOP) shows more of the eel's mouth, but the second (BOTTOM) shows more of the animal. Which one do you prefer? **Subject:** Moray eel. **Site:** Bonaire, Netherlands Antilles. **Equipment and film:** Nikonos RS, 50mm lens, Nikonos SB-104 strobe, Kodak Elite 100.

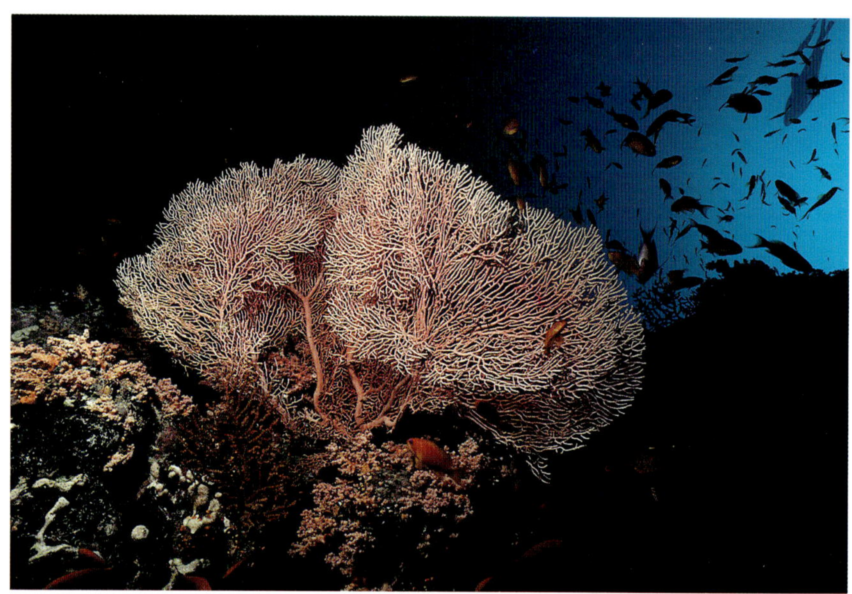

Checking all camera settings before you shoot will help to ensure a properly exposed picture. When shooting with a manual focus camera, extra care is needed when setting the distance scale on your lens because subjects look 25 percent closer under water, due to refraction. **Subject:** Sea fan. **Site:** Red Sea, Egypt. **Equipment and film:** Nikonos V, 15mm lens, Nikonos SB-103 strobe, Kodachrome 64.

Chapter 13: Think Before You Shoot

A checklist to improve your chances of getting a great picture while you're under water, and a predive checklist to guard against mistakes *before* you're in the water.

Now that you are familiar with the basics of underwater photography, you need to know one more thing: Think before you shoot.

Granted, in some cases you'll have only a few seconds to run through the list of all the things you have to think about before you press the shutter release button. However, utilizing these precious seconds to their best advantage will help improve your chances of getting a great picture. So, if you have time, think about the following items before you shoot.

Check camera settings: In all the excitement of the moment, it's important to check all your camera settings. Make sure the ISO dial, which you may have adjusted for a previous picture, is set at the proper film speed. Then, check your exposure mode dial, which can accidentally be moved when advancing the film winder on some cameras, to see that it's set for either automatic or manual exposure, whichever mode you prefer.

If you are shooting with a Nikonos V or Sea & Sea Seamaster Pro, adjust the focus, taking into consideration that a subject looks about 25 percent closer under water than it actually is.

Finally, check the LEDs (light-emitting diodes) in the camera's viewfinder. Make sure the under- or overexposure warning light is not on and, if shooting with a flash, make sure the flash-ready signal is lit.

Framing: Framing fast-moving and fleeting subjects—such as sea lions, sharks, and dolphins—is quite a bit different than framing an anemone fish on a stationary anemone or a grouper poking its head out of a hole in the reef. When photographing fast-moving subjects, you need to anticipate where the subject will be in the next few seconds. Granted, this is not as simple as it sounds. But, if you take your time, carefully watch the movements of your subject, don't frame too tightly, and follow the action like a cinematographer, you'll have a good chance of getting the shot you want.

When framing your subject, note the background, foreground, and all sides of the frame. By noting these areas, you can frame your subject so that the tip of a fin or a segment of anchor chain is not "peeking into the frame," thus ruining your picture.

Finally, remember that the subject does not have to be in the center of the frame for a good picture. In fact, an off-center subject "leads" the viewer's eye to the subject and creates movement in a photograph. The result is a much more dramatic effect.

Number of remaining exposures: Checking to see how many exposures you have remaining is a very important aspect of underwater photography, especially when you have those once-in-a-lifetime encounters. By checking the number of remaining frames, you can determine whether or not you have enough film to bracket, vary the flash position, and experiment with framing. If you have only three exposures remaining and know that the scene will be gone forever within the next minute, you need to run through the photo computer file in your head, call up all past underwater photo situations, make the necessary camera adjustments, and shoot. If you have followed the photographer's golden rule—Think Before You Shoot—you'll have a pretty good chance of getting an award-winning picture. Of course, a little luck won't hurt either.

Some things you don't want to think about: After you shoot, there are three things you definitely don't want to think about. "When I loaded my camera, did the film tab catch on the film take-up spool?" "Did I carefully replace all the O-rings after greasing them?" "Are my sync cords securely attached to both the strobe and camera?"

These simple procedures should be included in a predive checklist for all your underwater gear, including your camera rig. If you make a checklist and check it twice, you won't have to think about these things under water where you can't do anything about them.

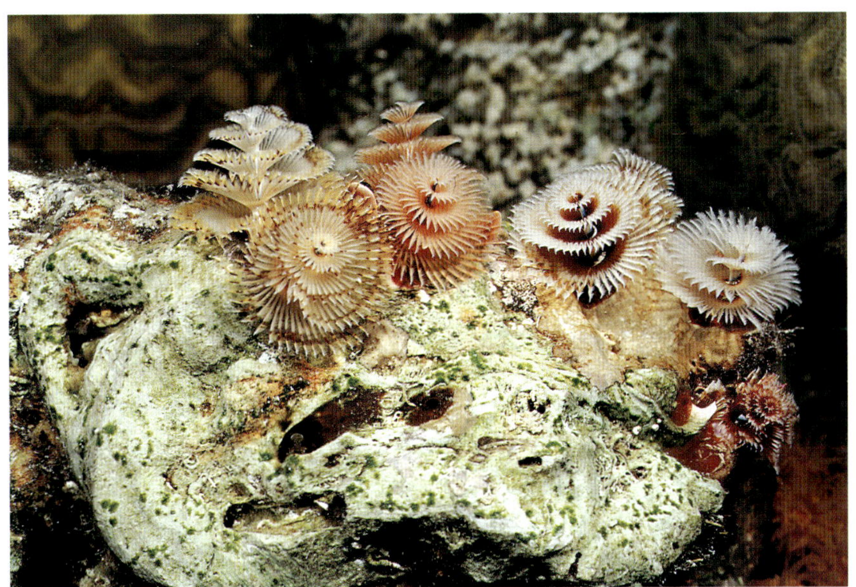

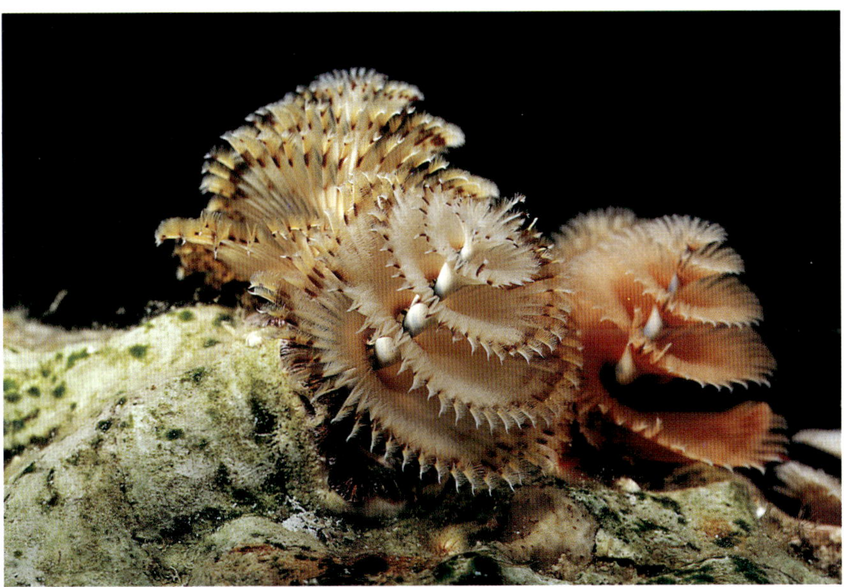

TOP AND ABOVE: Before you press the shutter release button, think about how the background and foreground can add to your picture. In the photo on the top, a busy background distracts from the main subject, the Christmas tree worms. In the bottom photo, which was taken at the same site but from the other side of the subject, an open-water background makes the subject stand out. **Subject:** Christmas tree worms. **Site:** Bonaire, Netherlands Antilles. **Equipment and film:** Nikonos RS, 50mm lens, two Nikonos SB-103 strobes, Kodak Elite 100.

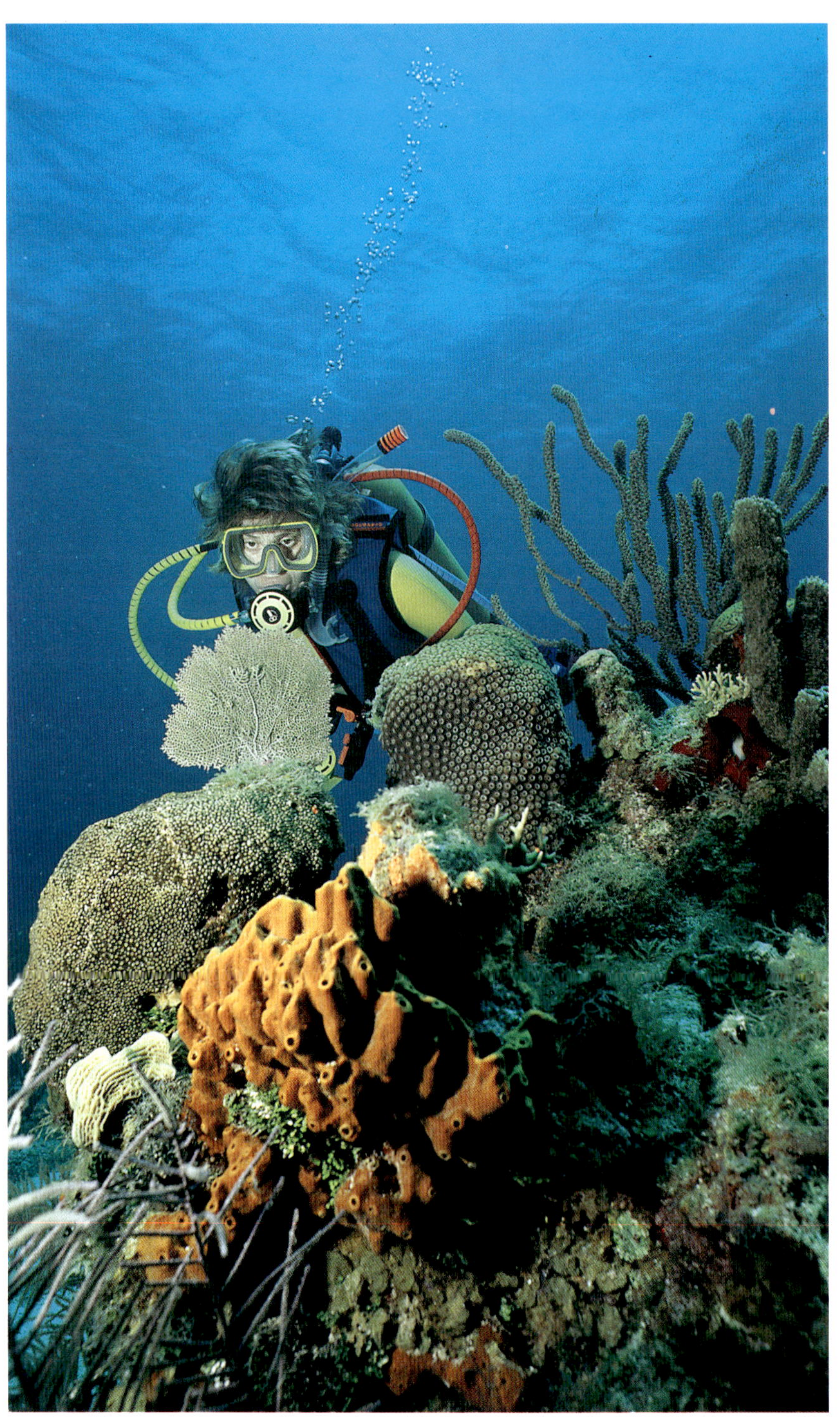

Chapter 14: Learn from My Mistakes

You can learn the hard way and make your own mistakes, or you can study these photographs and learn from them!

Making mistakes is part of becoming a good underwater photographer. And believe me, I've made *all* of them over the past fourteen years. However, although I admit to making mistakes, I can also say that I've never made the same mistake twice.

In this chapter you'll see some of my worst underwater pictures—pictures that were a result of mistakes that easily could have been avoided. Please study these pictures and read the captions carefully. By keeping my worst pictures in mind, you'll have a good chance of getting your best pictures.

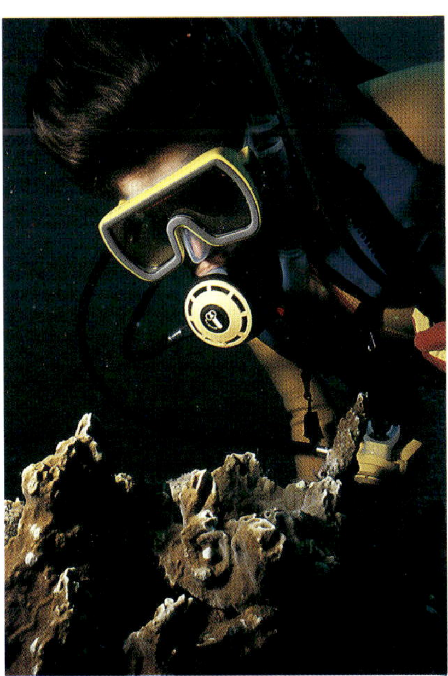

Problem: poor strobe position. When photographing divers, be sure to hold your strobe in such a way that at least some light fills your subject's face mask (LEFT). A modeling light on your strobe will help you accurately aim an off-camera strobe. Working with an experienced model or a dive guide will help you get natural-looking underwater portraits of divers (OPPOSITE).

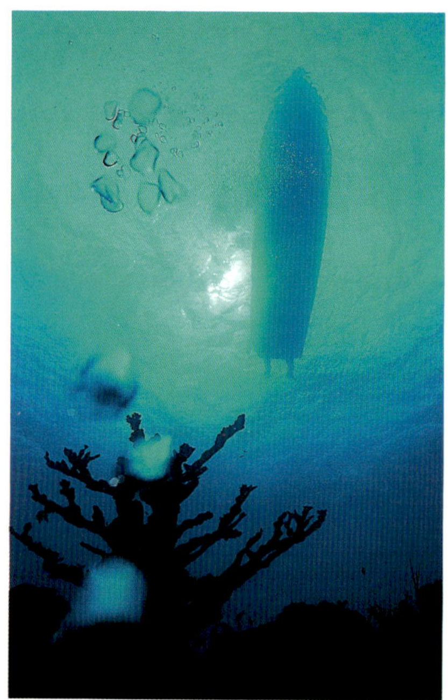

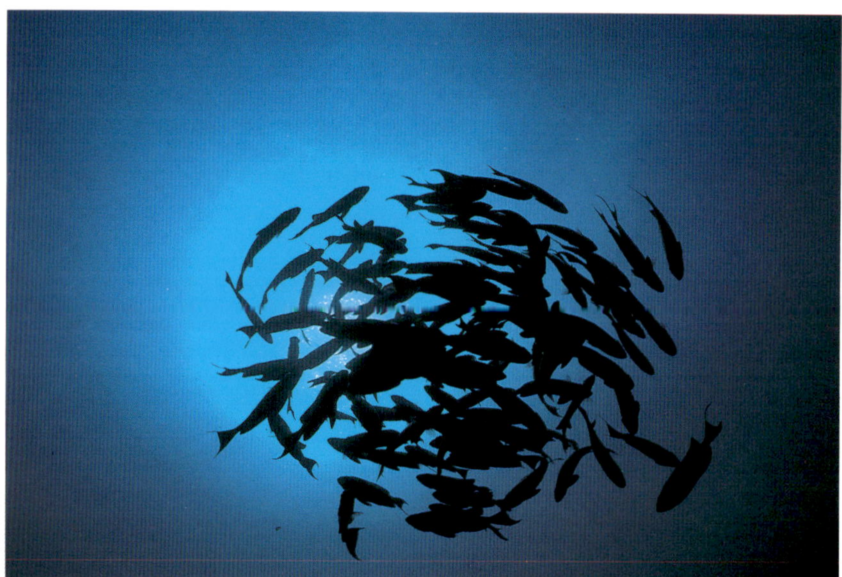

Problem: bubbles on lens. When you jump into the water, air bubbles can stick to your lens, ruining a picture (LEFT). So, before you shoot, wipe off these bubbles with a bare hand. Just seconds after I entered the water, this school of tangs began to circle over my head (BELOW). Luckily, I remembered to clean the bubbles off my lens before I pressed the shutter release button.

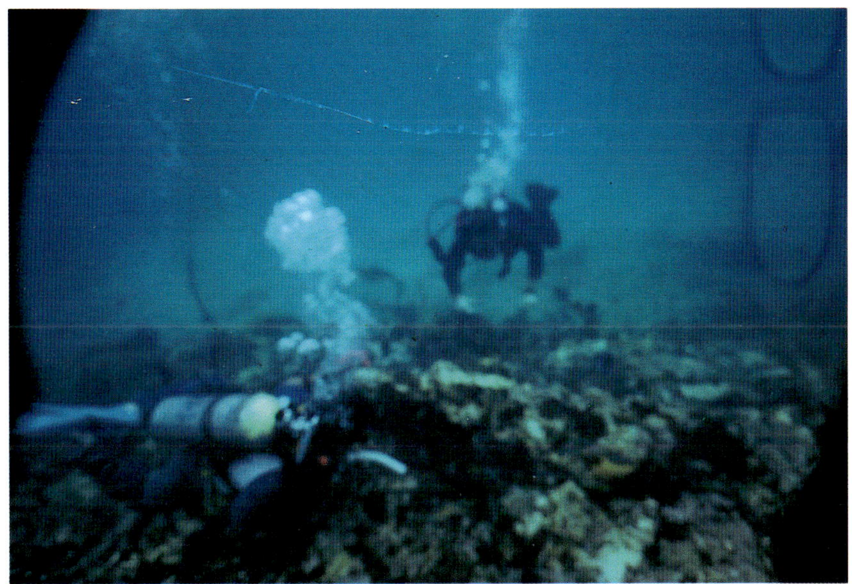

Problem: flooded camera. If you are not careful when greasing your O-rings, your camera can later flood, ruining your film, your camera, and perhaps your dive vacation (ABOVE). Spending fifteen minutes cleaning and regreasing my camera's O-rings was worth the effort for this Red Sea dive because the inside of my camera stayed bone dry (LEFT).

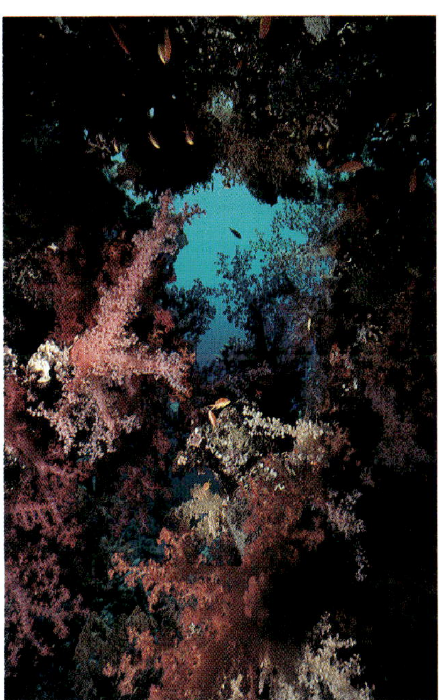

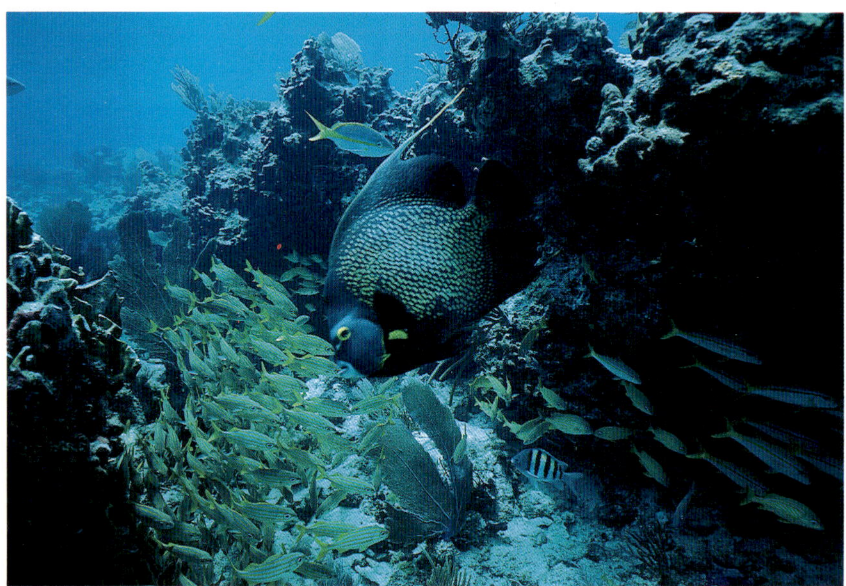

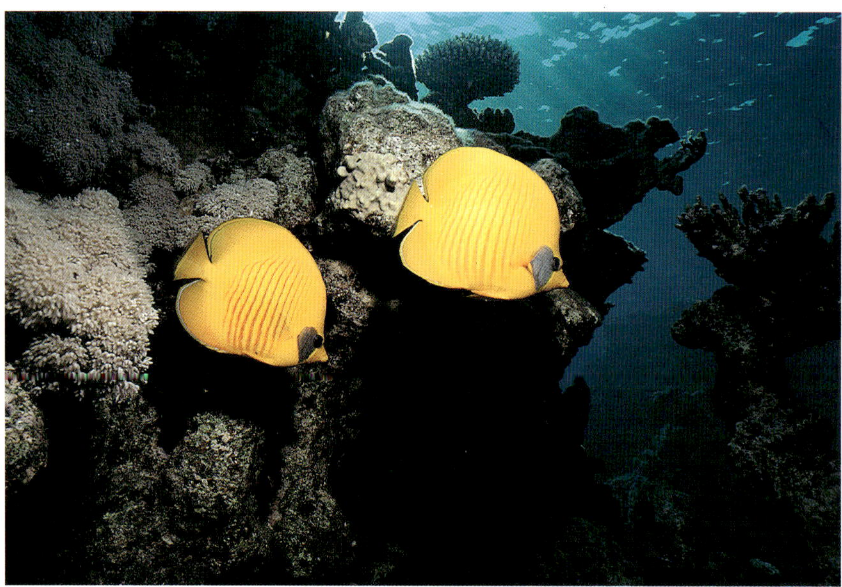

Problem: distracting wide-angle background. Background can make or break a scene. In this photo of an angelfish (TOP), the fish in the background ruins the picture. (The angelfish is not eating one of the yellow tail snappers—it just looks that way.) Cropping tight to highlight the beautiful color of these blue-cheek butterflyfish in the Red Sea, I swam with these fish until they were positioned against a plain background (ABOVE).

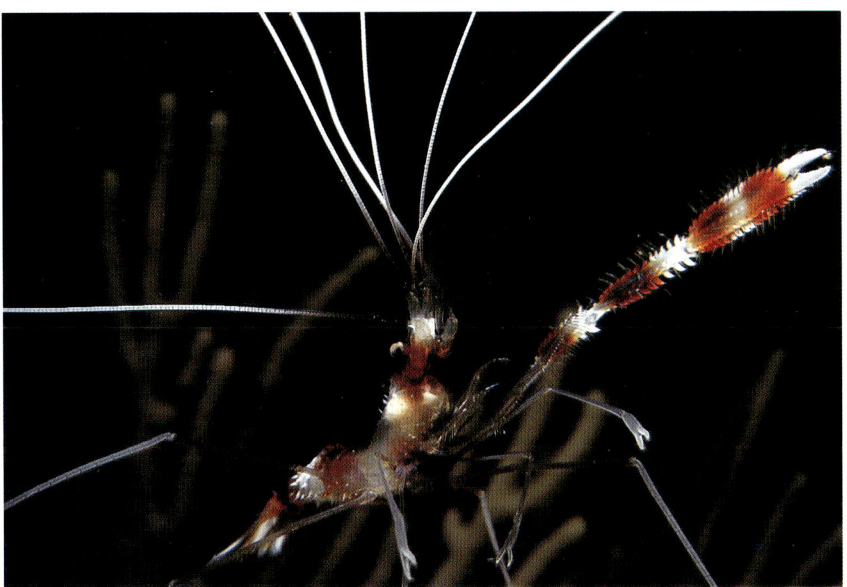

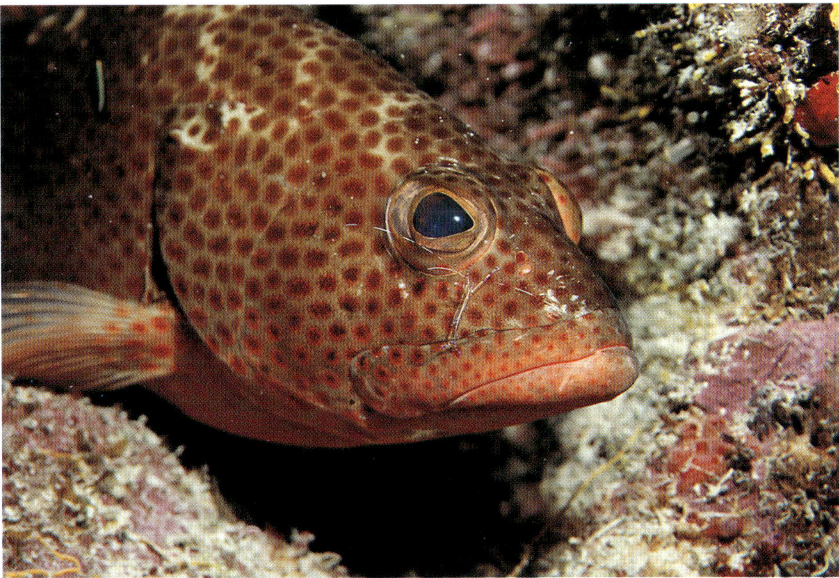

Problem: distracting close-up background. In macro photography, it is easy to concentrate on only the main subject, especially at night (TOP). When shooting close-ups, it is especially important to compose your scene with a plain background. This grouper was positioned against a busy background (BOTTOM), but I reduced the "clutter effect" by shooting at a wide *f*-stop, which produced shallow depth of field.

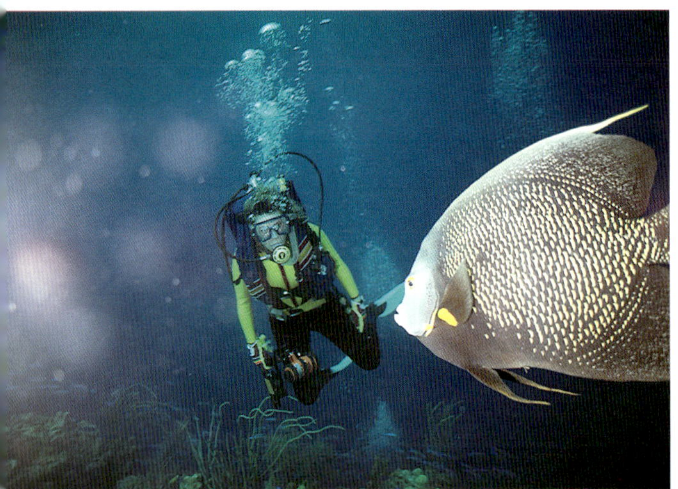

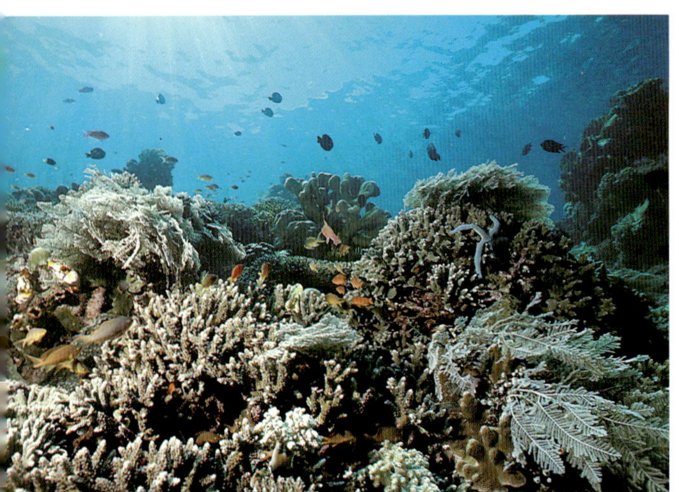

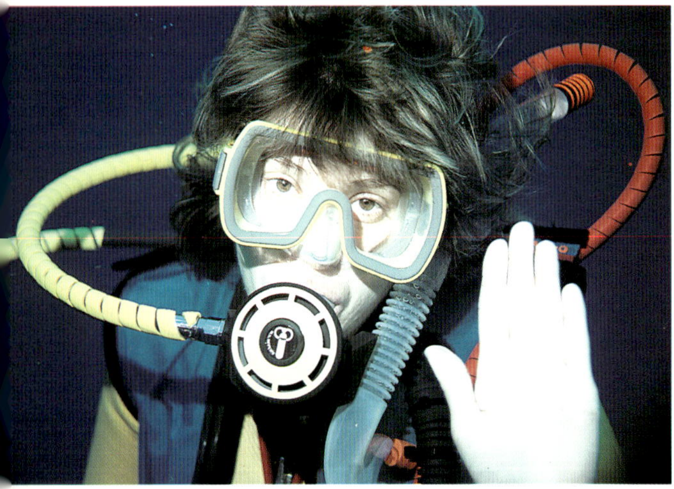

Problem: backscatter. Light reflecting off particles in the water resulted in these ugly blobs in my frame (TOP LEFT). Backscatter can be eliminated by holding the flash off-camera. As illustrated in this early morning scene on the Great Barrier Reef (MIDDLE LEFT), backscatter can be completely eliminated if the strobe is placed off-camera (three feet to the left in this case).

Problem: boring pose, poor exposure. Never have your subject look directly into the camera, or you'll get a silly-looking picture. Also, when taking a flash picture, make sure all elements in the scene are on the same plane, or that you expose for the closest subject. If you don't, at least one element (the hand in this picture [BOTTOM LEFT]) will be overexposed. Having a diver involved in an activity makes for much more interesting diver photographs. For added impact, have your subject aim a flashlight directly at the camera lens (OPPOSITE).

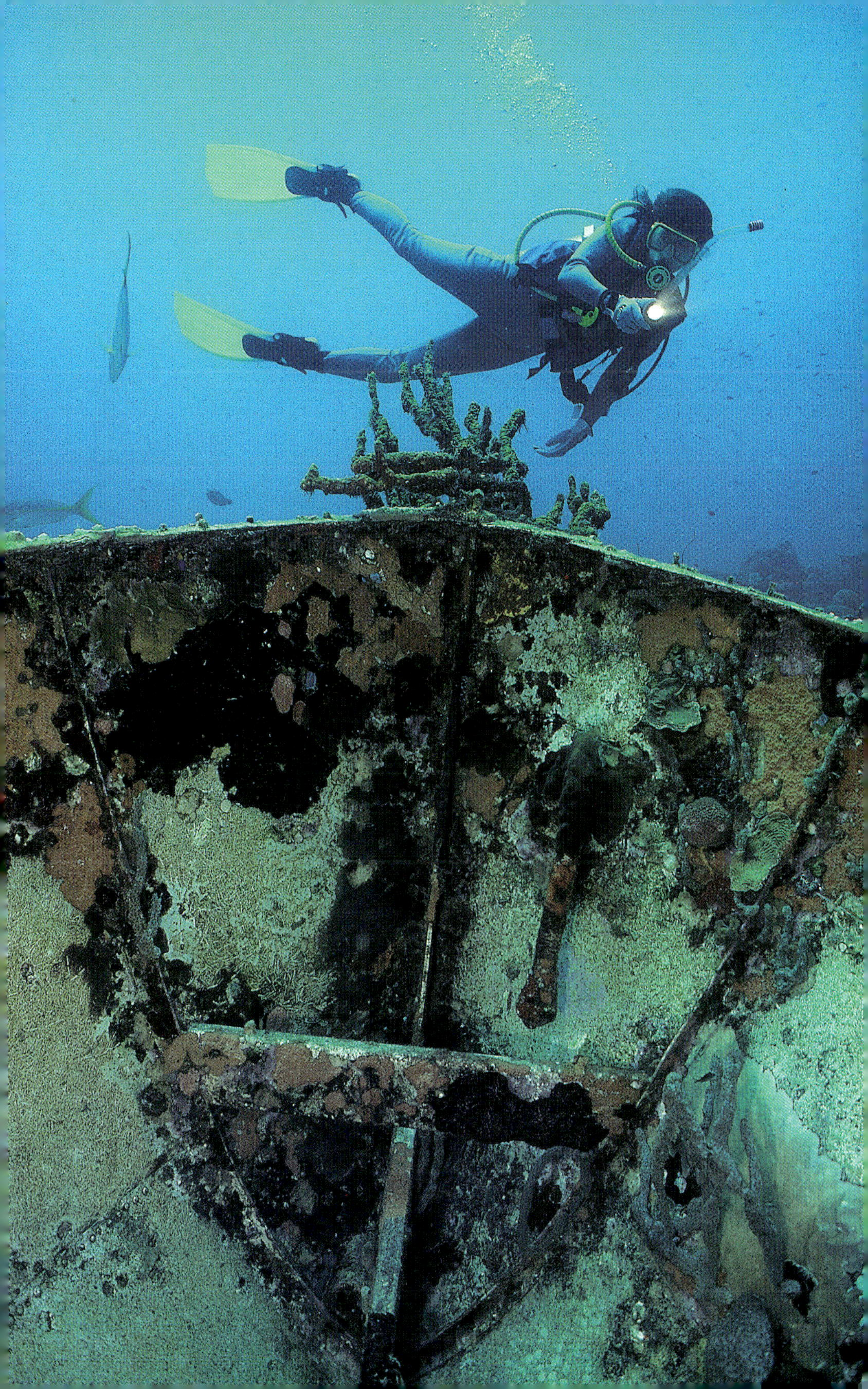

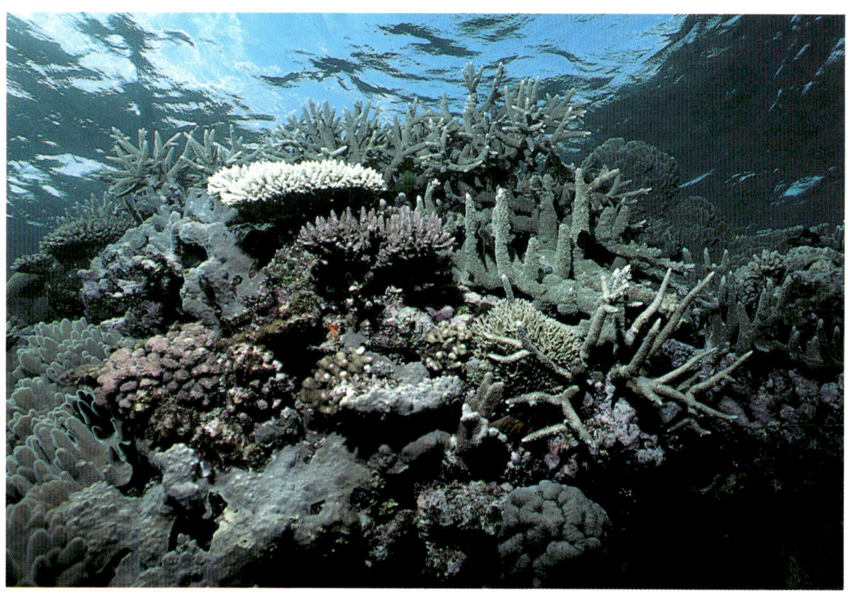

Coral reefs are susceptible to damage from divers and boats, as well as from pollution and changes in the environment. In fact, coral reefs the world over are in danger. On your dive trips, please remember that we are among the first generation to see the wonders of the underwater environment—let's do our best to make sure we are not the last. **Subject:** Hard coral garden. **Site:** Fiji Islands, South Pacific. **Equipment and film:** Nikonos V, 15mm lens, two Nikonos SB-103 strobes, Kodachrome 64.

Chapter 15: Preserve Our Underwater Wonders

"Take only pictures, leave only bubbles": Preservation of the underwater environment is vital, and it's your responsibility.

After reading this book, I'm sure you are anxious to "get wet" and start shooting some of the best underwater pictures of your life. But please remember, we all must respect the reef. It's a very fragile ecosystem whose balance is easily upset.

The reef is composed of millions of coral animals. These animals have a skeleton on the exterior of their body. Soft corals look more like plants than animals, while hard corals look more like rocks than animals. Both types of corals provide food for fishes and invertebrates. To help preserve our underwater wonders, please:

❊ Don't touch the corals when taking a picture, even though you may be tempted to do so for stability. If you do grab one, you'll wipe off some of the mucous coating that the coral colony uses to keep out predators and infection;

❊ Don't kick up sand after you have taken your picture. If too much sand settles on the corals, they can suffocate;

❊ Be aware of the corals when following the action in your camera's viewfinder. If you swim or float too close to the reef, you may accidentally break off a section of coral;

❊ Don't collect shells during your dive. Even empty shells are vital to the reef's survival. They provide homes for hermit crabs, fishes, and octopuses. In addition, algae, which is the food source for many animals, grows on shells. By removing shells, you are removing a food source from the reef;

❊ Finally, please remember the underwater photographer's creed: Take only pictures, leave only bubbles.

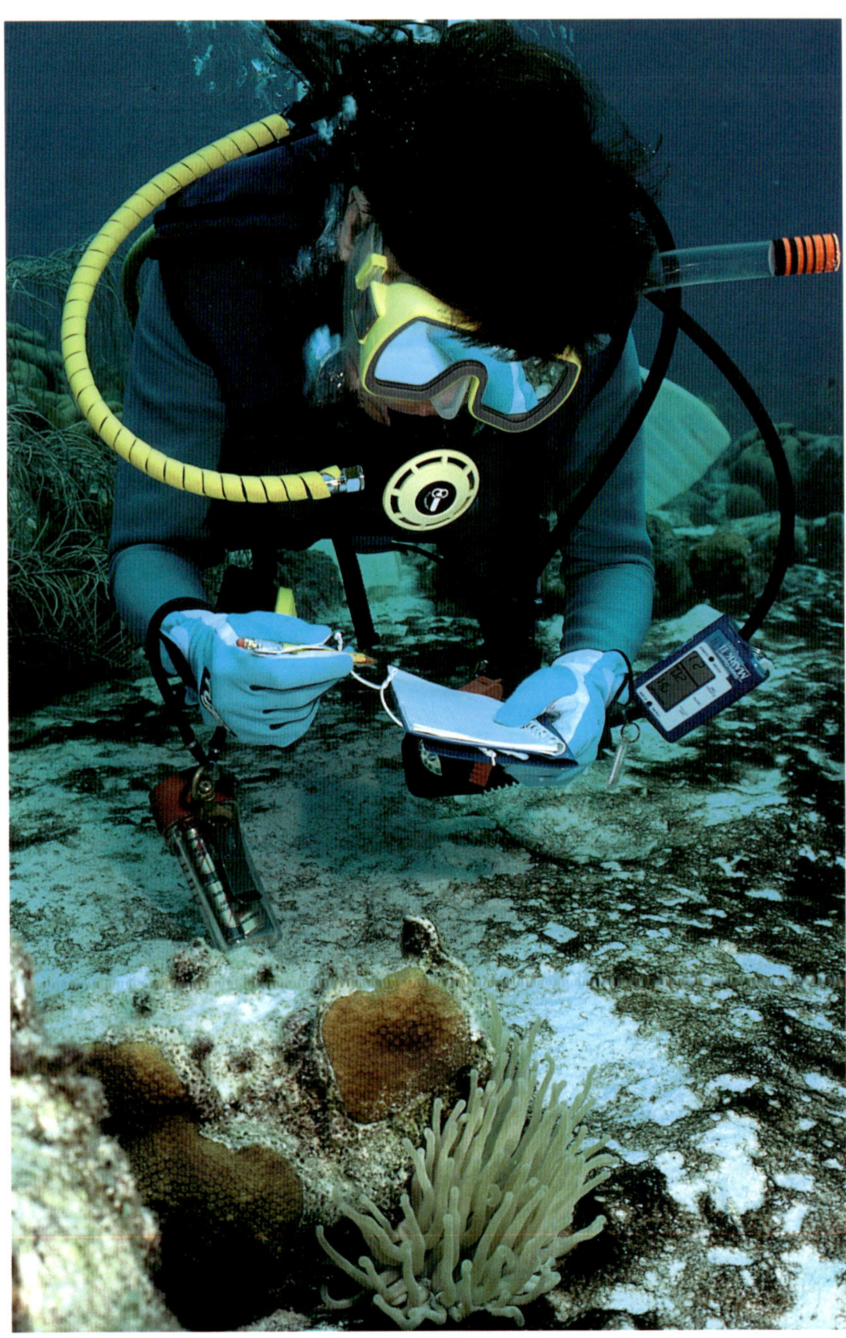

Adding a purpose to diving makes the experience that much more enjoyable. Here a diver is documenting the marine life on a coral reef with an underwater writing pad. **Subject:** Susan Sammon and sea anemone. **Site:** Bonaire, Netherlands Antilles. **Equipment and film:** Nikonos RS, 20–35mm zoom lens set at 20mm, Kodachrome 64.

Suggested Readings and Getting More Involved

Books, periodicals, and organizations that will make your dive trips more enjoyable.

To be a good underwater photographer, you need to be prepared when you arrive at your dive site, not only with the right equipment but also with some knowledge of what you'll find under water.

The following books will help you maximize your all-too-short time under water.

Best Dives of the Western Hemisphere, by Joyce and Jon Huber and Christopher Lofting. Published by Hunter Publishing, 300 Raritan Center Parkway, Edison, New Jersey 08818.

Greenpeace Book of Coral Reefs, by Sue Wells and Nick Hanna. Published by Sterling Publishing, 387 Park Avenue South, New York, New York 10016.

Encyclopedia of Aquatic Life, by Dr. Keith Banister and Dr. Andrew Campbell. Published by Facts on File, 460 Park Avenue South, New York, New York 10016.

Pisces Diving and Snorkeling Guides (available for Australia, Bonaire, California, Hawaii, the Florida Keys, Cozumel, and more), by various authors and photographers. Published by Pisces Books, P.O. Box 2608, Houston, Texas 77252.

Reef Creatures Identification (also *Reef Corals Identification* and *Reef Fish Identification*), by Paul Humann. Published by New World Publishing, 1861 Cornell Ring, Jacksonville, Florida 32207.

Seven Underwater Wonders of the World, by Rick Sammon. Autographed copy available through the author for $35.00. Write Rick Sammon, One Fox Road, Croton-on-Hudson, New York 10520.

This book will refresh your memory about, or introduce you to, basic photography techniques:

Camera Angles: Tips and Techniques for Professional-Quality Photographs, by Rick Sammon. Published by Voyageur Press, 123 North Second Street, Stillwater, Minnesota 55082.

To keep up-to-date on what's happening in the world of scuba diving, subscribe to:

Rodale's Scuba Diving magazine, 6600 Abercorn Street, Savannah, Georgia 31405.

Underwater USA magazine, 3185 Lackawanna Avenue, Bloomsburg, Pennsylvania 17815.

Eco-Tourism Photo Opportunities

The following is a list of some of the organizations that offer unique, educational expeditions for adventuresome photographers. If you want to put your photo skills to good use—perhaps for scientists who will appreciate your photos—send for information on these volunteer organizations.

CEDAM International, One Fox Road, Croton-on-Hudson, New York 10520.

EarthWatch, 680 Mount Auburn Street, Watertown, Massachusetts 02272.

University Research Expeditions Program, University of California, Berkeley, California 94720.

Glossary

AF (autofocus) sensor: A device in a 35mm SLR autofocus camera that tells the lens where to focus. Usually, the more sophisticated the camera, the more autofocus sensors it has. With additional sensors, arranged both vertically and horizontally, the camera can focus on a wide variety of subjects at different places in the viewfinder.

Aperture: The opening in the lens that regulates the amount of light that reaches the film. At the widest aperture (lowest *f*-stop number), the maximum amount of light reaches the film. At the smallest aperture (highest *f*-stop number), the least amount of light reaches the film. As the *f*-stop number increases (aperture decreases), depth of field increases (on all lenses).

Aperture Priority mode: Exposure mode in which you select the aperture and the camera automatically selects the shutter speed for correct exposure. Also called *aperture-preferred mode.*

Archival slide sheets: Chemically inert plastic slide holders designed to offer maximum protection for color slides. (Less expensive, nonarchival slide sheets can create a chemical reaction on the film and ruin your slides if stored for a long period of time.)

ASMP (American Society of Magazine Photographers): An organization for professional photographers which develops business guidelines for its members.

Automatic exposure: Takes the guesswork out of determining the exposure by automatically selecting the correct shutter speed and *f*-stop for proper exposure.

Autofocus: An optic-mechanical system that automatically focuses the lens on the subject.

Backlighting: Strong light from behind a subject that can create either a silhouette or an underexposed picture. Some cameras have a backlight compensation button, which automatically adjusts for this by increasing the exposure by about one and one-half stops.

Backscatter: Looks like snow in underwater pictures. Backscatter is caused by light from the strobe(s) reflecting off tiny particles in the water, and is reduced by placing the strobe(s) away from the lens.

Base plate: The tray of a strobe which allows the strobe to be attached to the base of the camera.

Bracketing: The technique of taking additional exposures of the same shot, under and over the recommended exposure settings—with the goal being a perfect exposure.

Camera shake: Caused by selecting a shutter speed that is too slow for hand-held picture taking, resulting in a blurred picture.

Close-up lenses: Inexpensive screw-on lenses that offer close-up possibilities for normal lenses (35mm to 55mm focal lengths).

Color shift: An unnatural shift in color that sometimes occurs during extremely long exposures (longer than one second).

Data back: A device with a variety of functions, including the imprinting of time and date on film. More sophisticated data backs also can control exposures and perform time-lapse functions.

Depth of field: The area that is in focus behind and in front of a subject. Sometimes called depth-of-focus. Depth of field is controlled by the size of the aperture, the focal length of the lens, and the distance between camera and subject.

Dive plan: A set schedule of activities that should be followed underwater. Remember: Plan your dive and dive your plan.

Exposure latitude: The measure of a film's forgiveness for over- and underexposed pictures. Slide films have a narrow exposure latitude, so your exposure must be as close to perfect as possible. Print films have a much wider exposure latitude, so you can take an over- or underexposed picture and still get a beautiful print.

Exposure modes: *See particular exposure modes.*

Extension tubes: Hollow tubes that are placed between the lens and the camera that increase the magnification and close-focusing distance of the lens. Used exclusively for close-up and macro photography.

F-stop: The various settings on a camera's aperture ring; these settings control the size of the aperture opening. The *f*-stop, or *f*-number, represents the relationship of the size of the aperture opening to the focal length of the lens. For example, an *f*-stop of *f*/16 on a 50mm lens means that the diameter of the aperture opening is 1/16 of the lens's focal length, or 3.125 mm. *See also* Aperture.

Fast film: *See* High-speed film.

Film speed: The measure of a film's relative sensitivity to light. "Fast films" (or "high-speed films") are very sensitive to light. "Slow films" are less sensitive to light. The speed of a film is represented by its ISO number. The higher the number, the faster the film. *See also* High-speed film; ISO number; Slow film.

Filters (color correction): In underwater photography, used to adjust color in a natural light scene or to balance the light from a flash to the color temperature of the daylight.

Filters: *See specific types of filters.*

Fish-eye lens: Produces a circular image on the rectangular frame. Has a field of view of 180 degrees and offers maximum depth of field.

Flash: *See* Strobe.

Flash sync speed: The highest shutter speed at which the flash is synchronized with the camera's shutter.

Focal length: The length of the lens, usually measured from the center of the lens to the film plane. For example, the focal length of a 100mm lens is 100mm.

Focus lock: A feature found on most 35mm autofocus SLRs that lets you lock in the focus of an off-center subject and then recompose the scene.

High-speed film: Film that is very sensitive to light; thus, it allows you to shoot at high shutter speeds to "freeze" action. Films with an ISO rating of 400 to 1600 are called high-speed, or fast, films.

ISO number: The film speed number. For example, Kodak Elite 100 has an ISO number of 100. (Previously, ASA *number.*) *See also* Film speed; High-speed film; Low-speed film.

LED: Light-emitting diode.

Lenses: *See particular types of lenses.*

Light meter: A device that measures the light level so the exposure can be adjusted either automatically or manually to the proper setting.

Low-speed film: Film that is not very sensitive to light. Low-speed films require slow shutter speeds; thus, when shooting with low-speed film, you may have to use a strobe. Films with an ISO rating of 50 or less are called low-speed, or slow, films.

Macro lens: A close-up lens, usually with a focal length from 50mm to 100mm. Lets you get life-size reproductions of small subjects.

Manual mode: An exposure mode in which you select both the aperture and shutter speed manually, to fine-tune your exposure.

Modeling light: Also known as an aiming light, a modeling light is in or on a strobe and allows the user to easily point the strobe at the subject.

O-ring: A round, rubber, gasketlike band that keeps water from leaking through the joints of cameras, housings, and strobes.

Program mode: An exposure mode in which the camera automatically selects both the aperture and shutter speed. Also called *Automatic mode.*

Remote control unit: A trigger-release device that allows you to trip the shutter from a distance.

Shutter Priority mode: An exposure mode in which you select the shutter speed and the camera automatically selects the aperture. Also called *shutter-speed-preferred mode.*

Shutter speed: The length of time the camera's shutter stays open when you take a picture. The shutter speed numbers represent fractions of a second; for example, with a shutter speed setting of 500, the shutter will remain open for 1/500 second when released.

Single-lens-reflex (SLR) camera: A camera that allows you to view the scene through the lens at the front of the camera and see the subject exactly as the camera sees it. SLRs offer a variety of interchangeable lenses and accessories.

Slave: A sensor on a strobe that fires the strobe when another strobe is fired.

Slow film: *See* Low-speed film.

Strobe: Another name for an underwater flash unit. Can be essential for bringing out the true color of underwater subjects.

Sync cord/connector: Connects a strobe to a camera (electronically).

Through the lens (TTL): Refers to the viewing mechanism of a camera. When you view a scene through the lens, what you see is what you get. With viewfinder-type cameras, you don't view the image area in exactly the same way as the lens sees it.

Wide-angle lens: A lens with a shorter focal length than a normal lens; thus it takes in a wide view.

Wire framer: Device used with extension tubes and close-up kits in which subjects can be placed for easy composition.

Zoom lens: A lens with variable focal length; thus it offers several lenses in one. For example, a 35–105mm zoom offers the shooting flexibility of a 35mm semi-wide-angle lens, 50mm lens, 80mm short telephoto lens, and 105mm medium telephoto lens.

Index

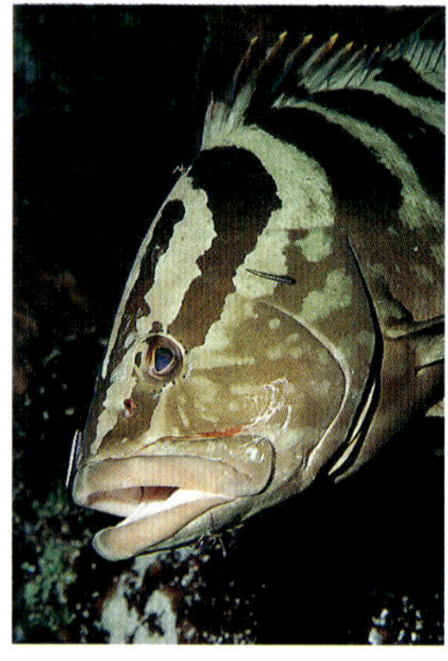

Where to go to find what you need to know.

About the Author

So what makes this guy qualified to teach about underwater photography?

The Complete Guide to Photographing Underwater Wonders is the first "how-to" book that takes all the guesswork out of taking pictures under water. Even beginning divers who have a basic knowledge of 35mm photography can get great pictures right from the start.

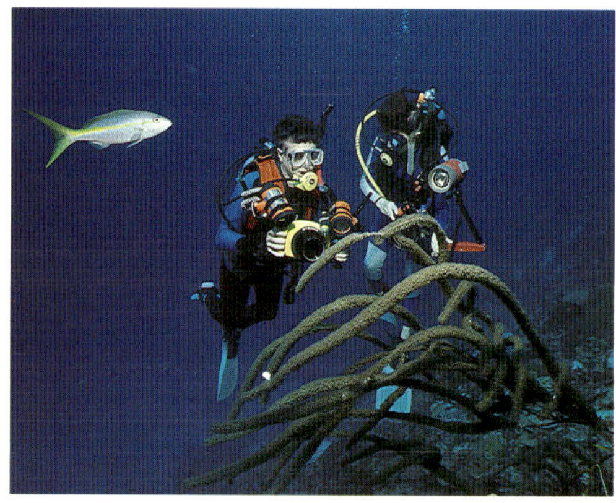

Photo by Angela Anderson.

Author Rick Sammon explains that with today's underwater cameras and accessories, it's really not that hard to get great pictures if you know the capabilities and limitations of the equipment, as well as the basics of shooting under water. As foreword writer Emory Kristof puts it, "A good guide is what is needed, and Rick Sammon is one of the best."

Internationally known explorer/photographer Rick Sammon has spent more than one thousand hours over fourteen years exploring and photographing the wonders of the world's oceans. Rick is one of the most published authors/photographers in the country. He has written more than a dozen books describing his experiences, including the award-winning international best-sellers *Seven Underwater Wonders of the World* and *Under the Sea in 3-D*. Two of Rick's recent books, *Camera Angles: Tips and Techniques for Professional-Quality Photographs* and *Hide and Seek Under the Sea*, are published by Voyageur Press. Rick also writes a how-to column for *Underwater USA*, a monthly newspaper-style publication for scuba divers, and is a contributor to Rodale's *Scuba Diving* and the *Explorers Journal*. He also writes a weekly photo column for the Associated Press, which is circulated to more than one thousand newspapers.

Rick is president and chief photojournalist for CEDAM International, a marine exploration organization dedicated to Conservation, Education, Diving, Archeology, and Museums. On CEDAM International expeditions, families can participate in marine conservation efforts. You can contact CEDAM at One Fox Road, Croton-on-Hudson, New York 10520. He is also a member of The Explorers Club, which is dedicated to the spirit of exploration.

When he is not diving or teaching underwater photography in the field, Rick can be found at scuba diving conventions, giving seminars on photography and marine conservation.

Rick's wife Susan is his underwater assistant. According to Rick, "half the credit of my photos goes to Susan, who not only helps me with my camera gear, but is an excellent critter spotter. Without Susan, I certainly would get a much lower percentage of great shots."

Also available from Voyageur Press

Hide and Seek Under the Sea, by Rick Sammon. A children's photo book of coral reef predators and prey and the amazing tricks they use in their fight for survival. (ISBN 0-89658-254-X)

Camera Angles: Tips and Techniques for Professional-Quality Photographs, by Rick Sammon. Straightforward and engaging advice from "America's most popular photo expert." (ISBN 0-89658-235-3)

The Art of Outdoor Photography: Techniques for the Advanced Amateur and Professional, by Boyd Norton. ". . . brimming with ideas, clever techniques, insights and encouragement. . . ." *The New York Times* (ISBN 0-89658-159-4)

Boyd Norton's PhotoJournal, by Boyd Norton. "There is no better way to learn photography than to keep a technical diary of what you shoot." *Outdoor & Travel Photography* (ISBN 0-89658-126-8)

Photographing Wildflowers, by Craig and Nadine Blacklock. "Excellent color illustrations and equipment/lighting diagrams round out a direct, strong presentation . . . " *Booklist* (ISBN 0-89658-069-5)

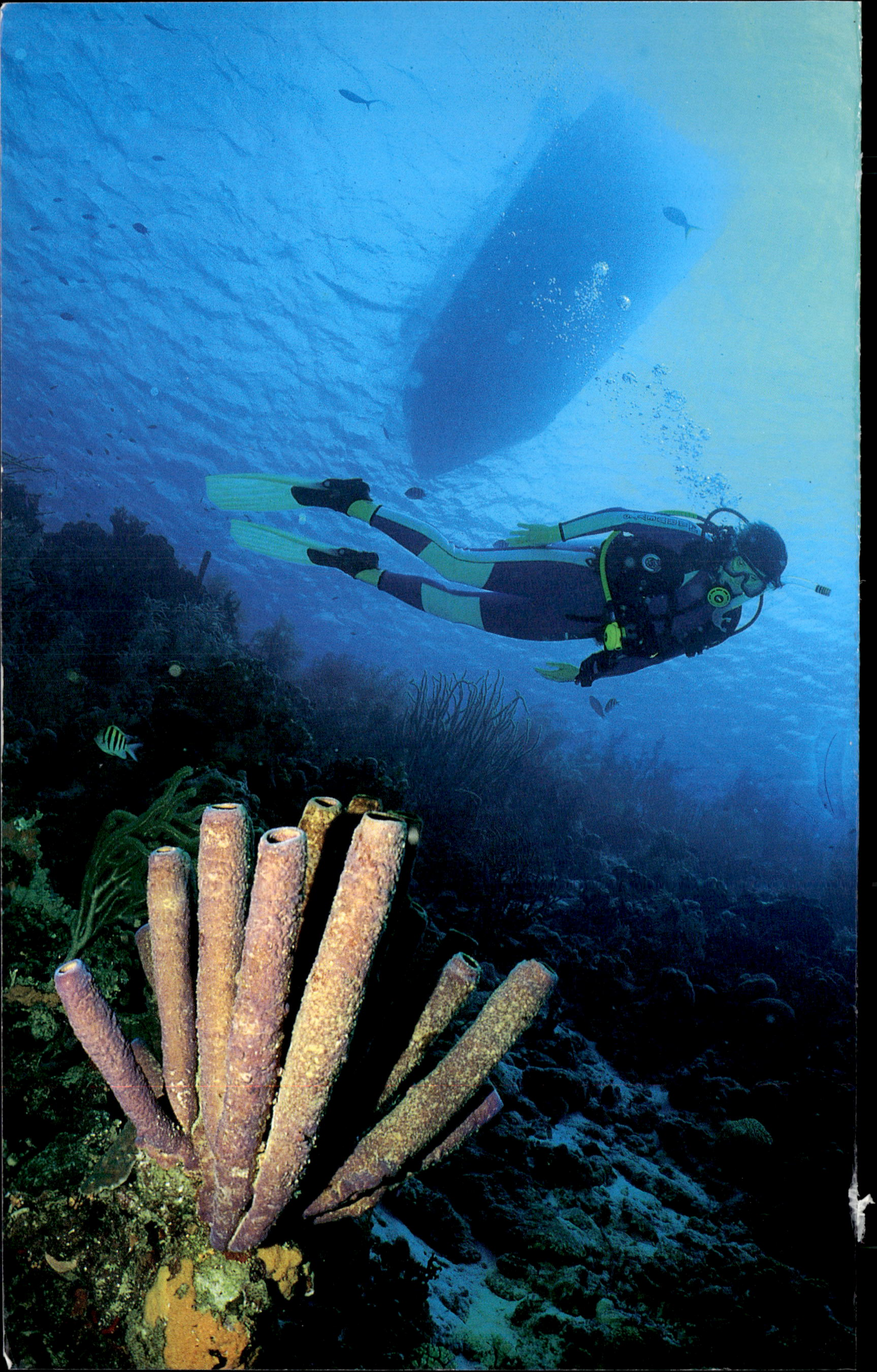